God, Man, & Well-Being

Nicholas Capaldi
General Editor

Stuart D. Warner
Associate Editor

Vol. 8

PETER LANG
New York • Washington, D.C./Baltimore • Bern
Frankfurt am Main • Berlin • Brussels • Vienna • Oxford

DOUGLAS J. DEN UYL

God, Man, & Well-Being

SPINOZA'S MODERN HUMANISM

PETER LANG
New York • Washington, D.C./Baltimore • Bern
Frankfurt am Main • Berlin • Brussels • Vienna • Oxford

Library of Congress Cataloging-in-Publication Data
Den Uyl, Douglas J.
God, man, and well-being: Spinoza's modern humanism / Douglas J. Den Uyl.
p. cm. — (Masterworks in the western tradition; v. 8)
Includes bibliographical references.
1. Spinoza, Benedictus de, 1632–1677. 2. Humanism—History. I. Title.
B3998.D395   199'492—dc22   2008006197
ISBN 978-0-8204-4462-8
ISSN 1086-539X

Bibliographic information published by **Die Deutsche Bibliothek**.
Die Deutsche Bibliothek lists this publication in the "Deutsche
Nationalbibliografie"; detailed bibliographic data is available
on the Internet at http://dnb.ddb.de/.

The paper in this book meets the guidelines for permanence and durability
of the Committee on Production Guidelines for Book Longevity
of the Council of Library Resources.

© 2008 Peter Lang Publishing, Inc., New York
29 Broadway, 18th floor, New York, NY 10006
www.peterlang.com

All rights reserved.
Reprint or reproduction, even partially, in all forms such as microfilm,
xerography, microfiche, microcard, and offset strictly prohibited.

Printed in the United States of America

In Memory of My Father
One of the Freest Men I have known.

"The freest cause of all, and the one most suited to God, is the immanent."

—*Spinoza* (Short Treatise on God, Man, and His Well-Being)

Contents

A Note on the Texts Used   xi
Acknowledgments   xiii
Introduction   1

1. *Homo Politicus*   7

2. The Foundations of Activity   27

3. The Ethics of Activity   49

4. Freedom   73

5. Modernity, God, and Man   95

Conclusion   123
Notes   131
Bibliography   143

A Note on the Texts Used

There are a number of translations of Spinoza's works available in English. The one that is probably now considered the standard text for scholarly use is Edwin Curley's *The Collected Works of Spinoza* (Princeton NJ: Princeton University Press, 1986). For this project, however, I have chosen to use Samuel Shirley's *Spinoza Complete Works* (Indianapolis: Hackett Publishing Co. 2002). The main reason is that I find Shirley's way of turning a phrase smoother and somewhat less pedantic. For my purposes here, that reason seemed appropriate. However, in a long-standing issue in English translations of Spinoza, Shirley has chosen to translate *affectus* as "emotion." Curley—more properly, I believe—translates it as "affect." The term "affect" is more neutral and less likely to be connected to cognate terms that could be misleading, such as "emotional." Nevertheless, "affect" does not carry much meaning in ordinary usage, so I have usually retained the Shirley translation as it is, unless I felt "emotion" was particularly misleading in a given context. Since most of my references to Spinoza's texts are in the body of my text rather than in footnotes, I have also adopted, with some minor variations,

Shirley's abbreviations for these works and their parts, the relevant components of which are as follows:

Works of Spinoza

E	*Ethics* (followed by Arabic numeral for part and internal references)
Ep	*Letters*
KV	*Short Treatise*
TIE	*Treatise on the Emendation of the Intellect*
TP	*Political Treatise* (followed by a Roman numeral for the chapter, and Arabic for the paragraph)
TTP	*Theological-Political Treatise* (followed by a Roman numeral for the chapter)

Internal References Used

A	Article
App	Appendix
Ax	Axiom
Cor	Corollary
Def	Definition
Lem	Lemma
P	Proposition
Pref	Preface
Schol	Scholium

Acknowledgments

In a project such as this one, there are obviously a number of people who have been instrumental in helping it to achieve fruition. In the early stages of this one, for example, I am indebted to Lee C. Rice for his usual sage advice on how to proceed and for his continued mentoring with respect to my understanding of Spinoza. My long time friend and co-author on many other projects, Douglas Rasmussen, has probed me with questions and comments that contributed greatly to the final product here. Among those who assisted me in completing this work, I am most especially indebted to Nicolas Capaldi, the editor of the series of which this book is a part. Prof. Capaldi's faith and patience with me as we worked towards completion borders on the saintly and no expression of gratitude can suffice.

Because this book uses excerpts from two previously published articles and one additional unpublished paper, the conferences in which those papers were delivered were invaluable to me in the preparation of those manuscripts and their incorporation into this one. One article, "Autonomous Autonomy: Spinoza on Autonomy, Perfectionism, and Politics," was part of a Social Philosophy and Policy Center Conference and later appeared in their journal (*Social Philosophy & Policy*, Volume 20,

Number 2, Summer 2003 pp. 30–69). I am most grateful to those who attended the conference and made comments on the paper, but I am especially grateful to Ellen Paul for her editing work, which included numerous substantive comments on that paper. Parts of this article can be found in chapters 1, 3, and 4 to follow. The other published paper is "Spinoza and Oakeshott" which appeared in a volume entitled *The Intellectual Legacy of Michael Oakeshott* (Corey Abel and Timothy Fuller eds., Imprint Academic (Exeter: 2005), pp. 62–85). I wish to thank the participants at the conference where the papers for that volume were first aired for their helpful comments, as well as to the editors of the volume, Corey Abel and Timothy Fuller. I wish to thank in particular Noel Malcolm who shared that particular panel with me and greatly enriched my understanding of Hobbes. Needless to say, I am most grateful to Imprint Academics for allowing me to reprint some of that paper here, mostly in Chapter 1. Finally, I delivered an unpublished paper entitled "Spinoza and Positive Psychology" at a conference on the "Philosophical History of Strengths and Virtues" at the University of Pennsylvania in September. 2004. The comments of the participants at that conference were most helpful, especially those of James B. Murphy. Besides the individuals already mentioned, I want to thank Elizabeth Hiestand for doing a first critical read and edit of the manuscript and then the staff at Peter Lang, especially Sophie Appel, for helping to polish off the rest. Last, but not least, I certainly owe thanks to my wife Margarita Molteni for giving me the time to myself to work on this instead of being of some help to her. Any virtues found in what follows doubtlessly owe their inspiration to all those just mentioned, while any faults must rest solely with me.

Introduction

It is hard to think of a figure more central to the rise of the modern world than Spinoza. Indeed, Jonathan Israel, in his massive studies of the Enlightenment, puts Spinoza right at the center of its most influential and revolutionary elements. In this respect, Spinoza, for Israel, is both the Enlightenment's most representative and its most influential thinker: "Spinoza and Spinozism were in fact the intellectual backbone of the European Radical Enlightenment everywhere, not only in the Netherlands, Germany, France, Italy, and Scandinavia but also Britain and Ireland."[1] Israel distinguishes between the modern and the radical Enlightenment with the former having the support of established institutions such as government, church, and universities, while the latter stood outside or in some other contrast to them. In the former camp were thinkers like Locke. In the latter, Spinoza. Both types of Enlightenment, of course, contributed to the success of the period and the ushering in of modernity; but it was the radical variety that marked the strongest impetus for change. The movement towards the modern world in which we now live was therefore fueled by controversies introduced mainly by the radical forces of the Enlightenment. If Israel is correct, not only is Spinoza the pivotal figure in the transformation of Western culture to what we now call the modern world, but we may still be grappling with many of the issues raised early on by Enlightenment thinkers such as Spinoza.

Consider, for example, Israel's description of what the radical Enlightenment was all about when it came to a number of issues central to debates of that time:

> The Radical Enlightenment, whether on an atheistic or deistic basis, rejected all compromise with the past and sought to sweep away existing structures entirely, rejecting the Creation as traditionally understood in Judaeo-Christian civilization, and the intervention of a providential God in human affairs, denying the possibility of miracles, and reward and punishment in an afterlife, scorning all forms of ecclesiastical authority, and refusing to accept that there is any God ordained social hierarchy, concentration of privilege or landownership in noble hands, or religious sanction for monarchy. From its origins in the 1650s and 1660s, the philosophical radicalism of the European Early Enlightenment characteristically combined immense reverence for science, and for mathematical logic, with some form of non-providential deism, if not outright materialism and atheism along with unmistakably republican, even democratic tendencies.[2]

This passage is remarkable both in its description of the modern world in which we now live and with respect to many of the issues that have remained issues for us over the last few centuries. If Spinoza was instrumental in giving life to these issues and attitudes, then the connection between Spinoza and the rise of modernity is clearly a profound one.

Yet to many what Spinoza's own doctrines are all about is not such a simple matter. Spinoza's "geometrical method" seems daunting and inscrutable. It proceeds like Euclidean proofs using definitions, axioms, proofs, scholia and the like to draw conclusions about the deepest and most abstract of topics, such as God, nature, matter, thought, knowledge, and freedom. Indeed, Spinoza's most important and famous work—*The Ethics*—begins by discussing the nature of God and the universe. Through the five books of *The Ethics* we begin with God and end with human freedom, with discussions of matter, thought, nature, knowledge, emotions, and the like coming in between. One of the main theses of the book is that there is no separation between

God and creation such that everything is a type of expression of God's nature and nothing stands outside that nature. The things that happen in nature unfold according to inexorable laws of thought and matter. Spinoza is famous for holding that there is only one infinite substance in the universe whose attributes, also infinite in number, include thought and matter themselves. From that infinite one substance the particularities we observe around us emerge.

From these few skeletal remarks one can already see the foundations for the controversies mentioned in Israel's passage cited just above. Not only is the traditional Judeo-Christian model of God and His created universe rejected, but that rejection is clearly coupled with a perspective on nature that we would now describe as scientific. The inexorable laws of nature call for explanations in terms of causes, not divine intentions or interventions. Moreover, given the scientific perspective, the quest for certainty at the human level moves us towards mathematics and away from theology. From the opening definitions, axioms, propositions and proofs of Spinoza's *Ethics*, the reader is drawn into this new framework for modernity.

The approach of many, if not most, authors who write about Spinoza is to follow him in the way he lays out his doctrine. Because that doctrine is presented as a consistent one, it seems necessary to explain Spinoza in roughly the order and topical approach he himself uses to present his philosophy. This is quite a plausible procedure, but one that is also as likely as not to lose the reader by its distance from our ordinary experience. For what one comes to realize is that the topics to be explained are not only of significant depth and complexity, but also presented in significantly abstract form as well. The truly interesting implications of the doctrine for our ordinary experience are thus difficult to extract.

Perhaps even more important is the fact that *sub specie aeternitatis* (from the standpoint of eternity), the human realm by Spinoza's account is a small and insignificant one. The universe does not revolve around us, and its vastness suggests that we are little more than a blip within it. Consequently, from a Spinozistic perspective, narrowing in upon the human realm could be considered something of a distortion of Spinoza's philosophizing and thus an approach to his philosophy that is askew at the outset. Consequently, most commentators (for good reason) spend the bulk of their time on the general components of the system and discuss the human realm as best as they can. Our approach in what follows is virtually the opposite of the usual one. We begin with politics and end with a brief introduction to Spinoza's metaphysics.

It might therefore be said that the discussion which follows is an attempt to understand, and thereby elevate, Spinoza's humanism. Apart from the need to have a task which is manageable, thus requiring some focus which inevitably risks distortion, a number of reasons seem to either call for or permit this approach. First of all, this work is part of a series devoted to discussing the ideas of thinkers who have been important to shaping our modern world. By virtue of the very nature of Spinoza's philosophy, almost any book one picks up on Spinoza accomplishes that goal as a matter of course. By concentrating primarily on the human aspect of Spinoza's thought, we hope to highlight a contribution to modernity that is much less recognized and, I believe, still under development.

Secondly, since this contribution to the series is meant to be nontechnical, it is hoped that by focusing upon the human we would draw the reader more readily into the thought of Spinoza and thus encourage a look at his wider philosophy. For if what Spinoza says about human beings is attractive, and his thought is largely consistent, then one's interest in the broader metaphysical issues is more likely to be engaged. Finally, this approach is not as inconsistent with Spinoza's project as first appearances suggest. For although we shall no doubt skim too quickly over some concepts that could use much fuller explanation, our point of focus may nonetheless be exactly Spinoza's own. Spinoza did write a book entitled *Ethics* suggesting an ultimate focus on specifically human development and conduct. Moreover, two of his other main works, the *Theological-Political Treatise* and the *Political Treatise*, are both about human issues of social and political life. Finally, another of his important works, *Treatise on the Emendation of the Intellect*, is about improving *our* understanding and is thus humanly focused as well. All this suggests that Spinoza too had the human world in center view.[3]

Although I hope that at least a few of the insights into Spinoza's humanism offered in the following chapters are relatively fresh, it is perhaps most unique to begin a discussion of Spinoza with his politics.

This topic, if discussed at all, is most often left for last and regarded as perhaps important to the history of political theory, but not much of an inroad to Spinoza's main philosophy. I shall in effect argue that it is more of an inroad than people suppose, because politics, unlike what one finds in most other humanistic theories, is actually not the place to find Spinoza's humanism. For that reason, the three chapters which follow the opening chapter on politics are devoted, in various ways, to discussing human well being according to Spinoza. Although "well being" is used in the title of the work of Spinoza's from which the title of this book is taken (*Short Treatise on God, Man, and His Well-Being*), the term I most often use in the chapters to follow is Spinoza's term "activity." These three chapters explore the various dimensions of living that are part of what it means to be active. One of the main points here is that the active life is possible for all, not just philosophers. But that life does not fit so neatly into the usual ethical categories prevalent today. On the one hand, for example, the doctrine as I interpret it is highly individualistic. On the other hand, the active life could not even begin to move forward without the help and presence of others. Similarly, much of what ethicists worry about—the obligations we possess whether defined by reason, socially established rules, or overall utility—seems less of a focus of interest for Spinoza than the promotion of the active life. While there is no pretense here of having covered every base on these questions of ethics and the nature of activity, it is nonetheless my hope that Spinoza will be seen a little less as a philosopher aloof from the human experience and much more attuned to what it means to live successfully in the modern world.

The final chapter says something about the metaphysical framework in which the earlier chapters must be set. Here the hope is that by looking at some of the main humanistic elements first, a greater understanding and appreciation of the metaphysical framework will result. Obviously, since something of a whole new door will be opened to the reader, a more complete examination of Spinoza's metaphysical principles will have to wait for later explorations. The doctrines one then discovers should, however, seem less distant and abstract given the approach I have taken here. The overall point of the last chapter is to discuss our place in the universe given the principles of activity that

I have enumerated earlier. Here we see an interplay between what I call immanence and insignificance that is a direct outcome of the kind of metaphysical system Spinoza develops. Insignificance is essentially our lot in the universe, but we can deal with its implications quite well if we strive for immanence. Immanence, as I use it here, is essentially another name for activity, but it has the advantage of being more descriptive of the process by which one becomes active, so there are certain contexts in which the word is helpful in understanding Spinoza's recommendations for human well being. If nothing else, the idea of acting from within ourselves as the chief characteristic of well being is perhaps best captured by the term "immanence."

In the end, then, my purpose is to treat Spinoza as someone who has something to say to us today. As one commentator on Spinoza has put it, "the true greatness of a philosopher rests not so much on the accident of his saying what he does at the historical juncture when he says it…but in the kind of timelessness of the content of his thought expressed through the statements he leaves behind as a legacy for reflective minds."[4] It is certainly the case that Spinoza's philosophy has intrigued reflective minds for centuries now. The modest reflection which is to follow is but one among many such inspired accounts. It is thus but one bit of evidence that there are many more to follow.

Chapter One

Homo Politicus

"A man can be free in any kind of state."

—*Spinoza* Tractatus Theologico-Politicus

Aristotle famously tells us that we are political animals. By that he means not only that we find ourselves in and seek the company of others, but also that we are interested in normative principles of how we should be governed. We are also political animals for Spinoza as well, but for rather different reasons. For Spinoza we must be social beings because we are too weak to live alone outside of society. Our sociality in this respect does not, however, make us prone to reflection upon the rules that govern us. This is primarily because politics is not for Spinoza the province of reason as it was for Aristotle. The principles that govern us may accord with reason, but political actors are seldom moved by reason nor likely to engage in rational reflection upon the nature and meaning of political principles. We shall develop this point in what follows. Politics is the first and necessary step towards activity and remains a context in which all exercises of activity take place, but politics is neither a source of, or means to, human well-being for Spinoza. Understanding this truth is the main point of what follows.

Let us therefore begin by noting that there is, for Spinoza, no creature less introspective than political man.

> But men are led by blind desire more than by reason, and therefore their natural power or right must be defined not by reason but by any appetite by which they may be determined to act and by which they try to preserve themselves. (TP 2, 5)

Given this starting conception of man as a political animal, the question becomes one of whether politics perfects us or not. Aristotle would hold that it does. Spinoza's position is that it does not. To see this clearly, it is useful to compare and contrast Spinoza with someone with whom he is often easily confused and who would himself not be normally associated with perfectionist politics—Thomas Hobbes.[1] In this connection we are aided by some reflections on Hobbes and Spinoza found in Michael Oakeshott. Oakeshott notes that Hobbes is "the first moralist of the modern world to take candid account of the current experience of individuality. But it is clear also in Spinoza."[2] Oakeshott also notes, however, that "unlike Spinoza, who presents us with a universe composed of metaphysical individualities (man being only a special case of a universal condition), Hobbes's starting point as a moralist was the unique *human* individuality."[3]

What then does Oakeshott mean by "human" individuality as opposed to the "metaphysical" individuality of Spinoza? The answer seems to me to come in the following passages:

> In the morality of individuality ... human beings are recognized (because they have come to recognize themselves in this character) as separate and sovereign individuals, associated with one another, not in the pursuit of a single common enterprise, but in an enterprise of give and take, and accommodating themselves to one another as best they can: it is the morality of self and other selves. ... Moral conduct is recognized as consisting in determinate relationships between these individuals, and the conduct approved is that which reflects the independent individuality understood to be characteristic of human beings. Morality is the art of mutual accommodation.[4]

And again:

> By the morality of individuality I mean, in the first place the disposition to make choices for oneself to the maximum possible extent, choices concerning

activities, occupations, beliefs, opinions, duties and responsibilities. And further to approve of this sort of conduct—self-determined conduct—as conduct proper to a human being, and to seek the conditions in which in may be enjoyed most fully. It is this approval—not merely on one's own account but in respect of others also—that the impulse towards individuality becomes a moral disposition. This is how human beings ought to live, and to be deprived of this exercise of individuality is recognized not only as the greatest unhappiness but also as the diminution of moral stature.[5]

What Oakeshott is apparently denying to Spinoza, and what also answers our question of what it means to be human, is the idea that individuals recognize themselves as such, both when reflecting upon themselves and when thinking of their relations with others.

Oakeshott's other intuition, that Spinoza was indeed one of the first theorists of a real individualism, is quite correct. The problem, and thus the difference between the two thinkers, then, goes back to the issue we have already raised—namely, what is sometimes termed "perfectionism." Perfectionism in the political context is the idea that politics or the state can and should play a significant role in "perfecting" us as human beings. I am suggesting that Spinoza is not a perfectionist in politics, but Hobbes to a limited extent is. That apparently small difference dramatically affects the understanding of the path to activity that will occupy us throughout the remaining chapters.

For Hobbes, politics begins with individuals. They are self-contained choosers who are self-aware of their own individuality as units of moral value and moral worth. However perverse, weakened, and combative, the parties to the original social contract for Hobbes see themselves as individual agents in the "human" sense given by Oakeshott above. They contract as moral equals, one among others, for the partial relief of their condition. They have no a priori expectation that they are inferior to anyone else, though they take their own desires more seriously than they do those of others. And it would be hard to make sense of the "sufficient signs" needed for a social contract to take root in Hobbes unless there was some mutual recognition of autonomous agency—that is, individuality.

For Spinoza, by contrast, "individuals" in something close to Oakeshott's sense only exist insofar as they are the adequate causes of their own conduct, which is to say insofar as they live by reason alone. Prior to that, they are pushed and pulled by forces outside their control and understanding. Consequently, it is more accurate to say that individuals do not exist in politics for Spinoza in the "human" or moral sense Oakeshott gives them in his account of Hobbes. That is to say, there is no individuality. Spinoza's individuals have ontological status as foci of behavior, but their moral status as individuals, their individuality, comes only when they are living the life of reason (E4P66Schol. & P73Schol.). That life, as we shall see more completely, is well outside the political. It is best then not to think of politics as the interaction of independent rational moral agents, but rather as the impassioned exertions and repulsions of individuals responding to stimuli in their social environment.

The difference here is significant. An individual in the Oakeshott/Hobbes sense may be present in Spinoza's civil society, but that individual is so statistically insignificant as to warrant no place whatsoever in theorizing about that society. As a consequence, it is correct to say of Hobbes that by grounding politics in the moral centrality of the individual, Hobbes generates a form of political theory exhibited in later liberal thinkers such as Locke and Kant. Individuals for these thinkers have moral rights against each other, and make claims upon one another in light of these moral rights. Individuality foreshadows notions of autonomy that are so central to much of liberal politics. Political theory has, in this tradition, a moral core and purpose.

But since there is no individuality in Spinoza's politics—only individuals moved by various forces outside of themselves—there is in fact no moral core to the theory. The theory borders more closely upon the descriptive or what is better captured under the heading of "social science" than "political philosophy." There is no moral standard circumscribing the theory and giving events a moral significance. Cooperation may be the essence of politics for both Hobbes and Spinoza, but for Hobbes discrete moral units recognize the value of cooperation in light of their own awareness of themselves as centers of moral authority. In Spinoza, to the contrary, cooperation is achieved as an expression of an equilibrium of interactive forces. There is no real moral value to it, because the result is not necessarily the product of moral design or moral agency. What is striking about politics for Spinoza is its amorality. Individuals in some fuller moral sense must make themselves for Spinoza, and thus individuality cannot be at the core of politics. So for Spinoza, politics *ends* when we have the sort of individuals alluded to by Oakeshott above. For Hobbes/Oakeshott, individuality is where politics begins.

The absence of perfectionism in Spinoza perhaps marks the first manifestation of the tension between constructivist and non-constructivist approaches to modern political and social theory. Constructivist social or political orders are ones that claim that the order of society is or ought to be the product of some human design. Non-constructive social orders are those that claim that the order of society as a whole in the most important respect is not, or should not be, the product of some overall design or plan. The order that exists evolves from the interactions of persons within a framework of procedural rules. Markets are typical examples of non-constructivist social orders. Government planning is a typical manifestation of constructivism. One can see the appeal of both constructivist and non-constructivist approaches.

On the one hand, the "spontaneous order" market-like arguments that would characterize Spinoza's non-constructivist side carry with them a certain realism when examined in light of the diversity and complexity of modern life. On the other, it could be argued that at some point our planning or injection of an order based upon envisioned consequences is inescapable—even for markets—and thus is at root the most essential component of the political. I suspect for Hobbes, and many others, the Spinozistic story was simply too a-rational to accept. Such a position seems, in the end, too inhuman to accept—mainly because it seems to abandon the peculiarly human faculty of reason. That the order we find around us is, as it were, the product of blind impersonal forces seems hard to accept. But perhaps we should turn the matter around and notice that it is fortunate that despite the irrationality of people, order can be found in society. For the two alternatives to this— that everyone become a rational philosopher or someone commands our actions according to a grand plan—are either unrealistic (in the first case) or antithetical to personal freedom, autonomy, and liberty (in the second). We can have a realistic perspective on human beings and have order and personal freedom too. As we shall see, what we cannot do for Spinoza is find our salvation in the political order.

The idea that politics begins in individuality has been at the center of liberal political philosophy since the time of Hobbes. Since it turns out that Spinoza is also a "liberal," it is tempting to attribute liberal political values to him as well. One commentator, for example, says the following about Spinoza's politics:

> Spinoza endorses the democratic republic because it is the regime most consistent with the autonomous individual or liberated self. Democracy is desirable because it fosters the conditions for reason and the expression of the individual.[6]

The same commentator also tells us, however, that Spinoza's notion of ethical perfection is "deeply antipolitical" looking instead to a "deeply private or solitary idea of the philosophic life, for which the requirements of political rule are inappropriate."[7] These potentially conflicting perspectives bring us to the problem of the individual and the individual's relationship to political life, namely, if individual perfection is so deeply antipolitical in Spinoza, then how can it be said to function centrally in politics or a political theory? On the other hand, perhaps if the state can "foster conditions for reason" and indeed exists to serve such a purpose, then as the foregoing passage implies, individual perfection could be at the very center of Spinoza's political philosophy.

My position is that individual perfection (or activity) is indeed deeply antipolitical, though not necessarily because it is solitary or contemplative. Rather, and most simply, it is because the political is very limited in scope for Spinoza and always and inherently appeals to what is passive and not active in human nature, whatever pretenses and accordances it may have with activity. Political action is never *active* in Spinoza's sense, and the effort to make it such carries with it confusions that can translate into social conflict. Politics for Spinoza has a simple limited function that in itself has nothing to do with perfection, activity, or blessedness. In this respect, the perfectionist politics attributed to Spinoza is a kind of confusion of reason with what accords with reason. The best we could say is that "democracy" does not contradict the perfected active life—not that it fosters it. To foster it would mean we would have some clear conception of how to bring activity about through political means; but that would be odd, since activity, as we shall see, is something that comes from within and not from without. Politics is always concerned with what is "outside" of us, in the ordinary sense of always operating in the public forum and in the technical Spinozistic sense that is connected to passivity. Of course, we can make the case negatively and say that "democracy" leaves those who are active free to be such. That is certainly true, and certainly something Spinoza in a normative posture would advocate. But we must remember that democracy also leaves people free to be passive and could be fully functional and successful in the absence of *any* active participants. Therefore, we would be equally entitled to say that democracy encourages passivity; but if it encourages both activity and passivity, it is either trivial or contradictory.

The problem is that one cannot approach Spinoza in ways traditional to political philosophy, that is, by holding to a normative ideal and then measuring the state against it. Spinoza's liberalism, for example, is not the point or purpose of his theory, but the consequence. One does not advocate liberal democracy to protect autonomy, but rather in the presence of liberal democracy, autonomy is protected.[8] Like everything else in Spinoza, if something acts from its nature, then it possesses the most power it can. When the state acts in accordance with its political nature, it too will maximize its power and effectiveness. As it turns out, states acting most in accord with the nature of the political are liberal states. And because the liberal state is the most effective employment of political power, we may wish to advocate it. Our advocacy of the liberal state, however, is not a reason for its superiority or its legitimacy. Rather, its superiority and legitimacy is our reason for advocating it. But we are beginning to lapse into paradox, so let us regroup and support some of our foregoing claims.

That Spinoza separates activity from political participation seems clear enough. We find, for example, statements like the following from the TTP:[9]

> Honesty and sincerity of heart is not imposed on man by legal command or by the state's authority. It is an absolute fact that nobody can be constrained to a state of blessedness by force or law; to this end one needs godly and brotherly

exhortation, a good upbringing, and most of all, a judgment that is independent and free. (TTP VII)

In the TP also Spinoza makes similar remarks:

> Those who believe that ordinary people or those who are busily engaged in public business can be persuaded to live solely at reason's behest are dreaming of the poets' golden age. ... Freedom of spirit or strength of mind is the virtue of a private citizen; the virtue of a state is its security. (TP I, 5–6)

The foregoing attitude towards the political is illustrated as well when we come to the issue of God and religion. In chapter four of the TTP Spinoza distinguishes human from divine law and tells us that they have a different aim. Divine law is the love of God that stems neither from fear nor the "love of some other thing from which we desire to derive pleasure" but from knowledge which is "certain and self-evident." In this chapter of the TTP, Spinoza is trying to show that belief in historical narratives is not necessary for our supreme good, but he is at the same time demonstrating that fears and rewards do little for that end as well. Consequently,

> The things whose goodness derives only from authority and tradition, or from their symbolic representation of some good, cannot perfect our intellect; they are mere shadows, and cannot be counted as actions that are, as it were, the offspring and fruit of intellect and sound mind. (TTP IV)

Sacred rites, we are told in chapter five of the TTP, have nothing to do with divine law and "therefore do not contribute to blessedness and virtue." Sacred rites are, in effect, political forms for Spinoza, since their object is obedience to some prescribed set of norms. This is equivalent to saying that politics—the pattern of stability established by obedience—has nothing to do with virtue or moral excellence.

There are, however, passages in Spinoza which seem to lend some support to a strong perfectionist reading. The most compelling one I can find goes as follows:

> So when we say that the best state [*imperium optimum*] is one where men pass their lives in harmony, I am speaking of human life, which is characterised not just by the circulation of the blood and other features common to all animals, but especially by reason, the true virtue and life of the mind. (TP V, 5)

If the best state were one that exhibits the highest moral excellence, it would seem that such a condition, within practical limitations, would be Spinoza's model for all political orders. Of course, it is logically possible for this passage not to contradict the others mentioned above, if "best state" is interpreted to mean what is desirable for "society at large" and not as a statement about political ends or processes. I believe that is the interpretation one must adopt to reconcile all the passages, and I shall argue for it below. If I am correct, we have the basis for the standard liberal distinction between state and society.[10] In any case, the passages cited prior to the foregoing one are significantly more representative in Spinoza's political work.

In Spinoza's *Ethics*, E4P35 and a number of the propositions that directly follow, it also looks as though Spinoza is recommending a perfectionist politics through the promotion of reason. There he seems to say the more reason there is, the more likely we are to live in harmony. Yet even though an ideal order is envisioned, Spinoza clearly tells us in the scholium to this same proposition that "it is rarely the case that men live by the guidance of reason." Moreover, two propositions later in the second scholium to proposition 37 we are told, "Wrongdoing is therefore nothing other than disobedience ... and obedience is held to be of merit in a citizen because he is thereby deemed to deserve to enjoy the advantages of the state." Wrongdoing or sin has more to do with social disruption than anything like activity in the ethical sense, and what is "morally" meritorious seems so because of its contribution to social stability. Furthermore, in E4P40 where reason and harmony are all but equated, "good" (*bona*) and bad (*mala*) are made equivalent to concord and discord, which is some distance from blessedness in any contemplative sense. So Spinoza is not at all averse to mixing passivity with what accords with reason in such a way that it is difficult to tell when he is speaking of one or the other. We can see this point to a large extent in passages like the following:

> It is not, I repeat, the purpose of the state to transform men from rational beings into beasts or puppets, but rather to enable them to develop their mental and physical faculties in safety, to use their reason without restraint and to refrain from the strife and the vicious mutual abuse that are prompted by hatred, anger or deceit. Thus the purpose of the state is, in reality, freedom. (TTP XX)

Here not only does it appear that the state has purposes, but its main one seems to be to secure freedom. Yet "freedom" at the end of the passage is little more than the avoidance of physical conflict. I have argued elsewhere[11] that many of Spinoza's key normative terms in the political writings, such as "peace," "freedom," and "reason" all have roughly the same meaning—namely, cooperative and obedient (to the laws of the state) conduct. They are all, in other words, political synonyms for harmony and order. These terms, therefore, do not necessarily have the same meaning in the political writings that they might in the *Ethics*.[12] "Freedom" in the political writings, for example, does not refer to "freedom" as activity found in books 4 and 5 of the *Ethics*. One can therefore be free in the political sense and yet be completely passive from an ethical perspective. The state "promotes" freedom when it is orderly and free of discord. Its members need not be free in the ethical sense. The same is to be said about "reason" which gets an edified rendering in the latter books of the *Ethics*, but takes on its rather mundane meaning of cooperation in the politics. In this passage "reason" *may* refer to that exhibited by the active person, but it need not, and in any case preventing fighting and quarreling and establishing safety is clearly the main object of state action.

Yet although it may be said that politics has no direct connection with the promotion of ethical freedom, it may still be possible to assert that Spinoza believes that "participation in political life helps create conditions (i.e., stability) under which the higher goods, such as philosophy, can be realized."[13] Here a kind of indirect perfectionism obtains where the inability of the state to directly secure freedom, activity, or autonomy is set to the task of providing the conditions upon which these goods might flourish. It has, in other words, a society of fully free and responsible individuals as its object but lacks the appropriate tools to achieve *that* end directly. Of course, this itself is something of an admission, for it gives a significant role to something outside of the realm of the political. Yet even this mitigated indirect claim is, I believe, too much perfectionism for Spinoza.

The basis for my skepticism is found in the TTP where we are told that the objects of human desire fall into three categories: knowledge of primary causes, control of the passions, and security and physical well being (*sano corpore*). The objects of desire also seem to be ranked by Spinoza with the highest being the first mentioned, to the lowest being the third. Politics is only applicable to the last category.

> The means that directly serve for the attainment of the first and second objectives, and can be considered as the proximate and efficient causes, lie within the bounds of human nature itself, so that their acquisition chiefly depends on human power alone; i.e., solely on the laws of human nature. For this reason it is obvious that these gifts are not peculiar to any nation but have always been common to all mankind ... But the means that serve for the attainment of security and physical wellbeing lie principally in external circumstances, and are called the gifts of fortune because they mainly depend on the operation of external causes of which we are in ignorance. So in this matter the fool and the wise man have about an equal chance of happiness or unhappiness ... To this end, reason and experience have taught us no surer means than to organise a society under fixed laws ... (TTP III)

Political life is concerned with security and physical well-being. Even with this limited a function, it does not guarantee success, but it is certainly necessary. Politics is really not concerned with moral and ethical matters, since that falls into the categories of the first two goods. In this connection, and keeping in mind what Spinoza calls "fortune" in the above passage, he tells us later in the TTP that, "the happiness and peace of the man who cultivates his natural understanding depends mainly not on the sway of fortune ... but on his own inherent virtue" (TTP IV). If the realm of "fortune" is the realm of the political and limited to physical security and harmony in the sense of minimizing or eliminating violence, injury, and social discord, then we have the quintessential minimal liberal state.

But why should politics be limited in this way? Has our case for the liberal minimal state just described, that is one that distances itself from moral matters, really been proved? Is Spinoza really so detached as I have suggested from political attention to the development of virtue and the good social consequences that follow from it? Consider as a possible counter argument the following passage:

> He who seeks to regulate everything by law will aggravate vices rather than correct them. What cannot be prohibited must necessarily be allowed, even if harm often ensues. How many are the evils that arise from dissipation, envy,

avarice, drunkenness and the like? Yet we tolerate these, because although they are in reality vices they cannot be prohibited by legal enactment. Much more, then, should we allow freedom of judgment, which is assuredly a virtue, and cannot be suppressed. Furthermore, it can produce no untoward results that cannot be contained, ... by the magistrates' authority; not to mention that this freedom is of the first importance in fostering the sciences and the arts, for it is only those whose judgment is free and unbiased who can attain success in these fields. (TTP XX)

Consider also that when Spinoza discusses sumptuary laws in his later work, he indicates a favorable attitude towards political manipulation for ends other than mere security.

I therefore conclude that those vices that are prevealent in time of peace, and which we are now discussing, should never be directly prevented but only by indirect means, that is, by laying such a foundation to the state that most men—I won't say will be eager to live wisely, for that is impossible—will be guided by such feelings as will conduce to the greater good of the commonwealth. (TP X, 6)

In these passages, the idea of the state using its resources to manipulate people towards "higher ends" seems not to be rejected and perhaps encouraged. In citing such passages, I have tried to give an indication where those who wish to offer a more expansive view of the role of politics in Spinoza's political philosophy might find some support in the texts.[14]

For me, however, the passage which probably best expresses Spinoza's normative attitude about politics is the following:

For a state that looks only to govern men by fear will be one free from vice rather than endowed with virtue. Men should be governed in such a way that they do not think of themselves as being governed but as living as they please and by their own free will, so that their only restraint is love of freedom, desire to increase their property, and hope of attaining offices of state. (TP X, 8)[15]

I believe this passage, coupled with some others I have cited, suggests strongly that some form of what is now called classical liberalism is Spinoza's political philosophy as we ordinarily think of "political philosophy." In no plausible interpretation, then, can there be a *direct* connection between autonomy and politics in Spinoza, for clearly politics is concerned with the passive side of human nature. The issue as we have seen becomes one of whether the state should seek to foster autonomy by indirect means and thus also hold it out as an end to be sought by governments and advocated by political philosophers. But having put the matter this way, the Spinozist should begin to feel that there is something wrong with the way we are now discussing the issue.

Spinoza finds it mistaken to begin with our preferred normative objectives and then spin out a political philosophy accordingly. The first chapter of his *Tractatus Politicus* is an indictment of this approach. Philosophers "conceive men, not as they are, but as they would like them to be." The result is that they have produced only political theory that "borders on fantasy, or could be put into effect in Utopia or in that golden age of the poets where there would naturally be no need of such" (TP I, 1). It is not just that philosophers are too idealistic and unrealistic. It is rather that they misunderstand the nature of the political by failing to understand that politics is either outside the realm of the moral and ethical altogether, or of such a limited connection to it that moral categories have little value when theorizing about it. This last point brings up an issue we cannot pursue here. Spinoza stands at the threshold of the development of modern social science. Social science seeks to give an impartial objective account of social institutions with normative conclusions and recommendations being given, if at all, only reluctantly, modestly, and "at the end" of the research. This is a point of procedure Spinoza emphasizes in the first chapter of the *Tractatus Politicus* (e.g., 4 & 5). I believe that Spinoza was engaged in an effort to undermine political philosophy as it was traditionally conceived and practiced and therefore as it may still be pursued today—namely, the sort which first paints the morally desirable order and then measures society against it. But it is outside the scope of this project to pursue that interpretation, or the more interesting questions surrounding the benefits and limits of such an approach.

Returning to the point that philosophers misunderstand the nature of the political, Spinoza tells us that the problem is with those "who believe that sovereign powers ought to deal with public affairs according to the same moral principles as are binding on the private individual" (TP I, 2). Now this statement brings us to an interpretative fork. On the one hand, given Spinoza's praise of Machiavelli, one could interpret this to mean that the moral rules which govern us privately do not apply to the public realm where violations of those rules might be necessary to maintain the regime. The other interpretation is the one I subscribe to. In this reading the problem is imputing to the sovereign functions it is not suited to perform, most notably the moral improvement of its subjects. Though Spinoza admires Machiavelli and his rejection of the utopian character of ancient political philosophy, he is not a Machiavellian in politics and does not advocate a two-tiered moral universe which allows for the abrogation of ordinary moral principles for political ends.[16] Indeed, almost the reverse is the case. If the political realm functions within its nature, those ordinary moral principles against theft, dishonesty, mutual harm, and the like are more likely to be secure and governing than otherwise. The problem comes when we ask politics to do more than that to which it is suited, and that is especially the case when we moralize politics beyond what is required for the simple peace and stability of the political order itself (TP I, 5).[17]

We are told by Spinoza that "a civil order is established in a natural way in order to remove general fear and alleviate general distress" and that this is a teaching of "reason"(TP III, 6). He then goes on to tell us that

> just as in a state of Nature ... the man who is guided by reason is most powerful and most in control of his own right; similarly the commonwealth that is based on reason and directed by reason is most powerful and most in control of its own right. For the right of a commonwealth is determined by the power of a people that is guided as though by a single mind. But this union of minds could in no way be conceived unless the chief aim of the commonwealth is identical with that which sound reason teaches us is for the good of all men. (TP III, 7)

But what could sound reason possibly declare to be good for *all* men, unless it is something fairly simple and basic and general? In answering, one must keep in mind both that people are not guided by reason, and also that "if [a state] is to endure, its government must be so organised that its ministers cannot be induced to betray their trust or to act basely, whether they are guided by reason or by passion. Nor does it matter to the security of the state what motives induce men to administer its affairs properly, provided that its affairs are in fact properly administered. Freedom of spirit or strength of mind is the virtue of a private citizen: the virtue of a state is its security" (TP I, 6). Indeed, when it comes to politics, "the teaching of reason is wholly directed to seeking peace" (TP III, 6). So the state most in accord with reason and thus most possessed of its own power will be the one that limits itself to the maintenance of peace and stability.

Spinoza makes the point about the limited ends of the state being ones of peace and security many times, but puts it most succinctly when he states, "The best way to organize a state is easily discovered by considering the purpose of civil order, which is nothing other than peace and security of life" (TP V, 2). This statement not only includes the word "best" (*optimus*), but comes in a chapter where Spinoza is describing for us his *ideal* state. That strongly suggests that, kept within its proper limits of securing peace, the state so limited will be most fully possessed of its own right and acting according to its own nature. The entire fifth chapter is consistent with this principle except for section 5, where we have the passage cited earlier about how the best state is one where there is "true virtue and life of the mind." But since that sort of virtue is a "private virtue" and not a virtue of the state, Spinoza must be telling us that while it might be most desirable to live among persons of true virtue, this is quite a distinct matter from what is connected to politics.

We must conclude, therefore, by rejecting any sort of moralistic or perfectionist politics when it comes to Spinoza.[18] We cannot, in other words, endorse the indirect perfectionism mentioned earlier where "participation in political life helps create conditions (i.e., stability) under which the higher goods, such as philosophy, can be realized."[19] Such a statement is either trivially true—stability is necessary for virtually any good to be achieved, including philosophy—or its aspirations clearly go beyond the political. The tools of politics involve appeals to passive emotions, primarily hope and fear (TP V, 6). The "ends" of politics are uniquely and sufficiently served when these tools are used to secure peace and stability. There is nothing more for politics to aim at or encourage. We don't participate in political life to have a shot at the philosophical, but rather we participate so that we don't get beaten up by our neighbor.

But I myself have argued elsewhere[20] that the liberal state is also the most powerful one for Spinoza and expected to be such. Here I mean powerful in all senses: economically, culturally, intellectually, and militarily. The temptation is to turn such expressions into a perfectionist political program. We must, however, be careful of our logic here. That obtaining some set of conditions C makes some other set of conditions P possible, is not at all the same as saying that C functions to produce P or that C ought to function to produce P. Even if we expect C to produce P more often than not, it does not follow that C functions to produce P as a sufficient condition for P. And obviously, if C is a necessary condition, then there may be other necessary conditions. And even if C is the only necessary condition, it does not follow that C functions to produce P, since it may also be a necessary condition for Q. So while I do believe that Spinoza thought something like the liberal state would be coupled with more perfection (i.e., more activity, pleasure, and power) among its citizens than alternative forms of government, this is not perfectionist politics, because the failure to obtain (positive) state P has no bearing whatsoever on there being something amiss or absent in C.[21]

I suspect that the move to say that C exists so that P will obtain in reading Spinoza comes from a false analogy. Individuals can move from conditions of passivity to activity as we saw earlier. Though the temptation is strong[22] and controversy about it exists in the Spinoza literature,[23] we cannot say the same about the state. The state is not an individual and does not have ever-higher levels of perfection to attain. Individuals within a state can obtain more or less perfection and thus make the state a more or less desirable place to be, but beyond peace and security the state has nowhere else to go. This is why when C obtains P may not. Conditions of freedom not only provide the opportunity for self-perfection, but may also offer many incentives for it such that, if it is to develop at all or most fully, those sorts of liberal orders are its most fertile soil. But if it does not develop, it does not follow that the political order in question is acting any less in accord with reason or less in possession of its own right. Nor does it mean that the state has failed to achieve its purpose of moving people along towards the path of virtue. All it means is that the individuals of that state failed, for some reason, to transform the opportunities freedom provides into a community of more active agents. The most we could say is that the state makes virtue possible, but as we saw in our opening epigram, the link Spinoza draws between virtue and statecraft is so minimal that virtually any state could be said to do this.

The places where Spinoza occasionally mentions unity of mind or purpose are less than convincing as an argument for the state's being an individual. In politics, any unity of mind (or purpose) we seem to possess can never be anything more than a commonality of passion (TP VI, 1). The passions here are simple basic ones: "subjects are not in control of their own right and are subject to the commonwealth's right only to the extent that they fear its power or its threats, or to the extent that they are firmly attached to the civil order" (TP III, 8). The sense here is that because we must unify with passions, the simpler and more basic the better. Attempts to unify across the wide range of passions would seem to be a recipe for dissolution rather than unity. Moreover, no hope is given that we will be unified through reason as an individual might be. So rather than trying to make a case for the state's being an individual in Spinoza, it makes more sense to say, as he does, that the state might sometimes act *as if* it were of one mind (*una veluti mente*) (e.g., TP III, 7). What the state is really doing, however, is providing a structure for aggregating individuals so that conflict and strife among them is avoided and so that they can repel foreign aggression. Indeed, if we make the state an individual, we seem compelled to try to find its higher levels of perfection, since it would be a human or human-like entity. That project, I submit, has virtually no textual basis to support it and seems prone to speculative absurdities (e.g., "is the active state more blessed than the active individual?"). Indeed, if the state were an individual, we would expect the text to go well beyond issues of conflict avoidance to which Spinoza continually and perpetually returns in both political treatises. When he seems to be making a positive case for some end beyond simple security—as he does perhaps in the famous twentieth chapter of the TTP—he always returns to the main focus. This strongly suggests that any connection between politics and "higher ends" is at best only negative.

We have been cautioned by Spinoza that the rhetoric of autonomy, perfection, or activity in politics can present dangers. The main danger is the moralization of politics. Here too we face a fork in the road. Spinoza's realism as indicated in the preceding paragraphs will certainly be taken by many, not as a refutation of the role of autonomy and morality in politics, but rather as the throwing down of a gauntlet—one to be taken up by political and moral philosophers everywhere. What they might claim is needed is more, not less, influence by, and reflection about, morality in politics. While it is clear to me that Spinoza would be rather skeptical of that perspective, it has in no way been my intention to convert those who hold to it to some sort of Spinozism. Even less has it been my expectation that I could do so. My intention has been simple: to bring to light some challenges to the orthodox modalities of current political theory the reading of Spinoza inevitably engenders. Those challenges alone might be worth consideration, whatever might be one's final conclusions on the place of ethics in politics and political theory.

But a thinker must be judged not simply by the challenges posed, but also in terms of the role his theories play amid the pantheon of political philosophers and political philosophies. To get something of a handle on this, consider the following:

> The general view of personal competence of the ancient Greeks suggests the fragmented ego, the "divided self"—generally passive, with appetites, emotions, and intellect isolated as independent agencies on the battleground of the body, unintegrated by any coherent higher-order planner within the self. ... Certain exceptional people might achieve something close to the contemporary concept of developed ego strength (i.e., Plato's philosophical souls), but they were rare, exceptional, god-like—the natural rulers of society. Correlatively, Greek political theory understandably focuses on rule by the best.[24]

This passage is cited at length because of its similarity to a number of the points we have made about Spinoza. The classical perspective described here was countered by the modern where everyone is supposed to have those capacities for personal autonomy claimed by traditional liberals. Rule in the modern framework, then, belongs to no one by nature. Where does Spinoza stand? Active (autonomous, perfected) individuals, who are so rare and are the natural rulers in the account of classical political thought described above, are never called upon by Spinoza to rule. Activity is neither necessary for, nor advocated by, Spinoza as a criterion for rule. The rulers may be (and are expected to be) as passive as their subjects. Antiquity seems to hold that perfectionism in ethics is naturally coupled with perfectionism in politics. The lack thereof of significantly differentiated individuals in the equalitarian foundations of modern ethics tends towards a lack of perfectionism in politics, or at least to a level of "perfectionism" matched to the universally shared "capacities" of all. Either way, no one in modern thought has the right by nature to rule, because no one is better than anyone else.

Spinoza, by contrast, is clear that some people are "better" than others, yet does not accord them a special right to rule. Perhaps that is because activity is, after all, of little special value to politics. Viewed in this light, what we can say about Spinoza's place in the pantheon is that he takes the road less traveled: perfectionist ethics and non-perfectionist politics.[25] What perfectionist ethics means for Spinoza is the subject of our third chapter. Here we have learned to distance the ethical from the political in the very name of the ethical itself. Doing so, however, means that the responsibility falls more heavily upon the individual alone to pursue self-perfection. To understand that responsibility, however, requires that we understand the existential core in which self-perfection consists. That core is "activity." Activity versus inactivity is the fundamental "choice" left to us by the recognition that politics and society cannot perfect us. We must therefore understand something about the nature of activity before we can explore its ethical meaning. To that task we now turn.

Chapter Two

The Foundations of Activity

"Our freedom lies not in a kind of contingency nor in a kind of indifference, but in the mode of affirmation and denial, so that the less indifference there is in our affirmation or denial, the more we are free."

—*Spinoza* (Letter to William van Blyenbergh)

As we noted at the end of the last chapter, politics for Spinoza is not the medium through which one will achieve the self-perfective condition normally called "activity" in Spinoza's thought. We are certainly among others in a social and political setting, but the task of becoming active is one we must undertake singly as individuals. Since this is so, we must begin to come to some understanding of what it might mean to be active. Though activity is rare, one of the central principles behind all our discussions to follow is that activity *accords* with human nature. It is not an aberration of it, but rather its very exhibition. Thus to be active is to be human; it is human nature normally understood, though not necessarily statistically normal. That point will become clearer as we go along. Secondly, because activity is "normal," it is not the province of a special elite. It is a possibility open to all, or so I shall argue. Finally, activity is a life-affirming process in Spinoza. It is not a transcendent state or one meant to be practiced in seclusion from ordinary life. Activity is the human form of well-being applicable and open to all. In this chapter, we begin an appreciation of what activity could mean understood in terms of its being the normal state of human well-being. The chapters which follow simply continue that same spirit while offering some further elaboration on the meaning of well-being for Spinoza.

Spinoza's Positive Core

One way to begin to get an understanding of the core of the humanistic dimension of Spinoza's conception of well-being is to take some of our bearings from the contemporary movement known as "positive psychology."[1] The reasons for doing so should become evident as we proceed. So far as I know, there is no direct connection between Spinoza and the founders of positive psychology, and it is not my purpose to assert there is such a connection. Rather, I hope to use positive psychology to help illuminate the meaning of Spinoza's account of activity and to appreciate some of the contemporary dimensions of that concept.

My understanding of positive psychology is that while it does not in any way wish to diminish the work that has been done in researching and helping to cure psychological pathologies, its focus is upon the nature of healthy psychological conditions and the means to attain them. From this approach to human psychology we may infer the following: 1) human beings can and do attain conditions of psychological health; 2) that these are conditions or states of being against which pathological states are measured and understood as pathological—that is, the conditions described by positive psychologists as healthy are those that are used to determine what conditions count as deviant, unsuccessful, unhealthful, and thus pathological; and 3) that psychological health is not a phenomenon found in an exceptional few, but is a possibility for any otherwise normal person. Positive psychology seems to hold that people are "meant" to be psychologically healthy, just as people are "meant" to be physically healthy. That psychological health is normal conceptually, if not statistically, is no more unusual or problematic than that physical well-being is normal.

If the pathological is associated with disease of the organism and disease is itself linked to decline, decay, and death, then it would seem to follow that positive psychology would be concerned with life- producing, maintaining, or enhancing actions and conditions insofar as those conditions concern the psychological—which I take to be our mental and emotional lives. The term "positive" in "positive psychology" comes neither from an adherence to the philosophical school known as "positivism," nor from an allegiance to unguarded optimism, but rather from the idea that psychological life must be understood in terms of what belongs to its ability to succeed and flourish. Put another way, positive psychology understands a healthy psychological life in terms of what that life positively exhibits, and not in terms of what it lacks, what hinders it, what destroys it, or what suppresses it, except in so far as these "negative" factors help us better understand its positive nature. Positive psychology is life-affirming, not because it believes there is no disease or death, but because life itself is some sort of process of affirmative exertion. From the idea that life exerts itself affirmatively into its environment as a descriptive notion, lessons can be drawn about what may enhance or detract from that process—that is, what sorts of exertions are likely to be more or less successful. Success here could be defined either in terms of what maintains and furthers the exertions or a state of satisfaction and integration or both.

The case of positive psychology, then, is exactly parallel to the concept of physical health.[2] The general sorts of things that can be said about physical health can be said about psychological health. One would expect then that positive psychology would have a robust conception of psychological health, one that goes well beyond "states of mind" or "feelings." We can see this in the following description of the various levels of a healthy psychological life. Seligman puts it thus:

> The pleasant life ... is wrapped up in the successful pursuit of the positive feelings, supplemented by skills of amplifying these emotions. The good life, in contrast, is not about maximizing positive emotion, but is a life wrapped up in successfully using your signature strengths to obtain abundant and authentic gratification. The meaningful life has one additional feature: using

your signature strengths in the service of something larger than you are. To live all three lives is to lead a *full* life.[3]

The three levels of psychological well-being described here will be used as a framing device for the remarks that follow. The theory discussed, however, will be Spinoza's and not necessarily Seligman's or that of any other proponent of positive psychology.

It seems to me that what is central to Spinoza's conception of human psychology and the main basis of the link between him and positive psychology is E3P12 and 13. In E3P12 Spinoza says,

> The mind, so far as it can, endeavors to think of those things that increase or assist the body's power of activity.

And in E3P13 just following it, he says,

> When the mind thinks of those things that diminish or check the body's power of activity, it endeavors, as far as it can, to call to mind those things that exclude the existence of the former.

These propositions are themselves built out of prior ones, which apply to mind and body alike, namely E3P7 and P9:

> The conatus with which each thing endeavors to persist in its own being is nothing but the actual essence of the thing itself.

And

> The mind, both insofar as it has clear and distinct ideas and insofar as it has confused ideas, endeavors to persist in its own being over an indefinite period of time, and is conscious of this conatus.

These propositions, when taken jointly, not only give us Spinoza's famous concept of *conatus* (the force of being in all things), but in doing so reflect the central notions that life is an activity of positive exertion. By positive exertion I mean the process of endeavoring to extend oneself into one's environment. This is the essence of life for Spinoza—extended endeavoring amidst other extended endeavourers. I shall say more about ourselves in relation to others below, but considering just the agent, we see from P7 above that Spinoza's doctrine is *essentially* life-affirming. Were it not for the presence of other and contrary forces, life would persist indefinitely (E3P4).

Of course, E3P7 does not specify just living things, and to give an extended account of the differences in Spinoza between the living and non-living with respect to *conatus* would take us well beyond the scope of this chapter. For our purposes, the presence of an individuative mind is a key difference. There is first individuation itself, and then Spinoza's conception of the mind in relation to it. The mind is nothing but the idea of the body for Spinoza (E2P11–13) and if those bodily dispositions are integrated into an individual, so will the mind be to that extent. Spinoza discusses individuation in the Lemmas and Axioms following E2P13. Basically, if diverse parts can retain their relations while acting as a single exertion on surrounding forces and objects, the entity is an individual. The measure of success is the degree to which these various endeavorings remain integrated and proceed without obstruction.

Now if we leave out *a great deal* and cut to the main point here, we can see the connection between these baseline propositions and human flourishing or activity, if we add but one other significant proposition: "A free man thinks of death least of all things, and his wisdom is a meditation of life, not of death" (E4P67). The mind not only endeavors to persist, but when properly directed (i.e., when moved by what Spinoza calls "active" ideas, discussed below), it thinks about life- affirming things. Included in these life-affirming "thoughts" are emotions, as we shall discuss more fully elsewhere. We are not then, when "healthy" in Spinoza's system, caught up in negative thoughts, frames of mind, or emotions. Of course, no one escapes the negative at all times, let alone other forces in nature that impede our life functions. But Spinoza's overall suppositions are clearly positive and life-affirming while at the same time indicating that life-serving endeavors are in keeping with the dispositional essence of human nature.

The strong life-affirming or "positive" character found in Spinoza's philosophy would in turn seem to imply that the good would also have to be, in some form, practical, since it would be closely tied to *actions* that are life enhancing. There may be parallelism (between mind and body) in Spinoza, but there is not dualism. Consequently, there would be no *mental* health without physical correlates. I am not referring to simply "brain waves" but to processes within the human body as a whole and to human actions. A human being is still a living organism, which acts in its environment *as an organism*. It is neither stagnant nor, when healthy, fragmented or partial. What is "good" for it, then, is understood not in terms of some part of the organism—for the parts contribute to the whole—but to the whole individual. There are distinctions, but in the end there is no separation. The mind is the idea of the body and the emotions are not located in one or the other exclusively. This means, for Spinoza, that all the aspects of human nature are in systematic if not organic relationships with one another. Our mental, emotional, and physical lives are very much interconnected with each part affecting and depending on the others. Our task is to recognize this and to formulate patterns of action that maintain and further the integrity of the human organism as a whole. That is certainly a positive project.

For Spinoza successful living must be understood as having mental and physical descriptors of the very same actions and processes. The mental and physical are never detached, and while we might think of the extreme ends of a continuum of the mental and physical as bearing little relation to each other—that is, autonomic processes at one end and philosophical abstraction at the other—Spinoza denies even this (E2P12). The point, of course, is that given the nature of life and a non-dualistic assumption of the mind/body relationship, one would *expect* a strong correlation between mental and physical health as emphasized by positive psychologists.[4] But the first instance of that connection comes in the realm of pleasure to which we now turn.

The Pleasant Life

When discussing the elements that go into making up a full human life, positive psychologists speak of "the pleasant life," "the good life," and "the meaningful life." I believe it will be useful for us to adopt these divisions in our discussions to follow. The divisions correspond roughly to the three levels of the good in Spinoza that I shall speak about later. Moreover, given the humanistic orientation of this book, these categories are useful conceptual tools for organizing the various components of Spinoza's conception of activity. Although this chapter is entitled "activity," what we are doing here is laying the foundations for a discussion of activity which is finally only realized at the highest level or in a "meaningful" life. For the moment, however, we must concentrate on the first level of goodness for Spinoza, which is pleasure.

For positive psychology, "the pleasant life ... is wrapped up in the successful pursuit of the positive feelings, supplemented by skills of amplifying these emotions." In addition, "the pleasures are delights that have clear sensory and strong emotional components ... they are evanescent and they involve little, if any, thinking."[5] For Seligman pleasures, both bodily and "higher" pleasures begin with "joy" and then move outward from there in terms of the descriptors (e.g., bliss, rapture, gladness, glee, etc.) that are applicable to them.[6] And within the techniques of enhancing pleasure, savoring and mindfulness play important roles. Savoring is the awareness of pleasure and the deliberate conscious attention to the experience of it.[7] Mindfulness seems not much different to me than savoring, since it too is devoted to paying attention to the present experience of pleasure. But techniques for increasing the degree of mindfulness of a pleasure would undoubtedly enhance the degree of one's savoring. We might think, then, of savoring as the descriptive term having various degrees depending upon the amount of mindfulness present. The more mindfulness, the greater the savoring. Obviously savoring is experienced most fully from a perspective of mind/body integration.

Positive psychologists also draw an important distinction between pleasure on the one hand and gratification on the other. Basically "pleasures are about the senses and the emotions. Gratifications, in contrast, are about enacting personal strengths and virtues."[8] Gratifications are what move us from a life consisting simply of a string of pleasurable experiences to the "good life." Gratifications, then, are essentially the topic for our discussion in much of what follows in later chapters, but since I shall argue that a very similar and central distinction exists in Spinoza as well, it was important to introduce the notion here.[9] It is also important to note Seligman's description of gratification at this stage because it too will factor into later discussions. Seligman says,

> In contrast to getting in touch with feelings, the defining criterion of gratification is the absence of feeling, the loss of self-consciousness, and total engagement. Gratification dispels self-absorption... .[10]

As I shall argue below, the pleasure/gratification distinction is quite parallel to Spinoza's distinction between passive and active emotions. Indeed, there are a number of striking parallels between the pleasure/gratification axis in positive psychology and the approach taken to pleasure that is found in Spinoza.

Turning to Spinoza, his discussion of pleasure is interesting. Consider the following:

> We see then that the mind can undergo considerable changes, and can pass now to a state of greater perfection, now to one of less perfection, and it is these passive transitions that explicate for us the emotions of Pleasure and Pain. So in what follows I shall understand by pleasure "the passive transition of the mind to a state of greater perfection," and by pain "the passive transition of the mind to [a] state of less perfection." (E3P11Schol.)

Spinoza goes on to tell us that there are only three primary emotions: pleasure, pain, and desire. In E3P9Schol. he notes,

> When this conatus is related to the mind alone, it is called Will; when it is related to mind and body together, it is called Appetite, which is therefore nothing else but man's essence. ... Further, there is no difference between appetite and Desire except that desire is usually related to men insofar as they are conscious of their appetite.

Two other explanations of terms should be added here before we give a gloss on what Spinoza's theory may mean. The first is how Spinoza describes emotions. Spinoza defines "emotions" as "the affections of the body by which the body's power of activity is increased or diminished, assisted or checked, together with the ideas of these affections" E3Def.3. The second term we need to consider is "perfection." Spinoza says simply this of perfection: "by reality and perfection I mean the same thing" (E2Def.6).

Let's try to put some of this together, starting with perfection. By equating reality and perfection, Spinoza is referring to the degree to which something persists in being, or the power of its endeavoring or conatus. The more power something has to persist or endeavor, the more reality or perfection it has. A desire or pleasure would, therefore, have more perfection or reality the more it compels us, and less to the extent that it is easily altered or vanquished. Obviously linking perfection to emotion (understood now as pleasure, pain, and desire) could speak to the degree of perfection of the emotion, but notice that the definition of emotion is tied into the activities of body and mind. It is their activity to which terms such as perfection and reality are applicable, not simply to the "feel" or the state of being. This is important because there are different ways to effect the transitions.

There are many levels with which we could begin to undertake an analysis of the key terms we have mentioned above. These range from the biological to the ethical.[11] Our emphasis must be at the level of the person and the person's psychology rather than the many pre-and subconscious levels implied in Spinoza's conception of emotion. It is worth pointing out, however, that Spinoza did see emotions as very much a function of *all* activities going on in the body. As Antonio Damasio notes, emotions function as homeostatic devises for the body as a whole and thus must be in touch with all elements of it.[12] Our focus then must be on desire as Spinoza defines it above, for it is the conscious pleasures and pains that parallel what positive psychology is speaking of in the passages cited earlier.

It is interesting that Spinoza uses the term *laetitia* for pleasure and *tristitia* for pain. It can be argued that the better translation for *laetitia* is actually "joy"—the term with which Seligman begins his discussion of pleasure.[13] Furthermore, it turns out that joy is at the heart of the matter for Spinoza. Damasio again puts this point in a way that helps us link it to the definitions and proposition from Spinoza just cited.

> For Spinoza, organisms naturally endeavor, of necessity, to persevere in their own being; that necessary endeavor constitutes their actual essence. Organisms come to being with the capacity to regulate life and thereby permit survival. Just as naturally, organisms strive to achieve a "greater perfection" of function, which Spinoza equates with joy.[14]

Organisms tend to persist and to increase certain activities and avoid, desist, or reduce others. Conditions and responses to our actions that reinforce those actions tend to increase our endeavors in that same direction. It is natural to say about pleasure, for example, that the things we find pleasurable are things we desire to continue to pursue and the things we find painful are things we wish to avoid or reduce.[15] Our "reality" or "perfection" is thus enhanced and our endeavoring persists. Consciousness of the process may issue in the "feels" that we delight in and may wish to savor; but we should not confuse the symptom (the "feel") with the phenomenon itself (the endeavoring). Though Seligman speaks of the "symptom" in the passage cited earlier, there is no inconsistency here. The healthy organism, and thus the healthy mind, is one that finds ways to perfect its endeavoring so that there is in fact much to savor. For Spinoza we are, then, hard-wired for joy!

What is "good" for us and what we "like" would thus seem to be meant to have some connection with one another. That foundation is the idea that pleasurable desire is the basis for what can be called "good," and painful desiring the basis for what can be called "bad." Spinoza says the following:

> By "good" I understand here every kind of pleasure and furthermore whatever is conducive thereto, and especially whatever satisfies a longing of any sort. By "bad" I understand every kind of pain, and especially that which frustrates a longing. For I have demonstrated above (E3P9Schol.) that we do not desire a thing because we judge it to be good; on the contrary, we call the object of our desire good, and consequently the object of our aversion bad. (E3P39Schol.)

We are tempted immediately to dismiss the use of these terms "good" and "bad" as not being moral or ethical uses. In fact, however, this would be a mistake. Not all ethical philosophers are Kantians, so that the desirings that describe our nature also turn out to be the ones that provide the standards for our success and ultimately our fulfillment. That is, they have some bearing on what we *ought* to do. Spinoza *does* mean here not only that we pursue our pleasurable desires and call its objects good, but also that it is good that we do so, because what the good is, is this pleasurable striving. Ceteris paribus, we are recommending as well as describing here. Pleasure is good. Pursue it. While this is by no means the whole story, it is also a part of the story that never disappears from what would more recognizably be seen as ethical conduct.

So why is this not the end of the story? Why not say that we should pursue pleasure and then perhaps add a cooperative rider that we do so as long as we don't hurt others trying to do the same? Why, in other words, have we not finished giving a description of the good life—at least in Spinoza's case—when we've finally understood that there's nothing more than "enhancing perfection?" As it turns out there *is* nothing more than enhancing perfection, so far as mental health or ethical advice is concerned. The problem is that the story told so far may provide the structure of the theory, but some critical elements within that structure still need to be discussed. The most important of these elements is Spinoza's distinction between active and passive emotions.

What exactly is missing in the account we have been giving of pleasures and pains? The discussion lacks the more or less obvious issue of whether the direction in which we may be persistently endeavoring is the "right" one. For positive psychologists a life of only "positive emotion" would still be a life significantly lacking in some important ingredient of happiness. What would be lacking in that life is meaning, expressed earlier in the form of gaining gratification. But why isn't the life of "positive emotion" gratifying? Perhaps there is an answer that at one and the same time would explain why it makes sense to discuss both pleasures and gratifications in the same chapter—however disparate they seem to be—and at the same time indicate something Spinoza is driving at in his distinction between active and passive emotions. The answer, I believe, is a version of the old philosophical distinction between "what happens to one" and "what one does." The emotionally pleasant life is essentially a life that happens to one and not a life that flows from, or out of, what one is or what one is doing. In both cases it is still one's life that is the subject of the event, and in both cases the forms of endeavoring are positive. But the life of pleasure seems not to concern something we have brought about, but rather concerns something brought about within us. What positive psychology and Spinoza are both saying is that the meaningful life, the happy life, the good life, or whatever similar terms one wishes to employ, is a life essentially expressive of something that we do or bring about rather than about something we experience. Positive psychology refers to this act or doing as a function of exercising one's "signature strengths," which first requires an identification of what those strengths are and then puts them to use in such a way as to increase "flow."

The Good Life

It is important to begin this section by noting that the good life, however different it may seem in description, is never cut off from the "pleasant" life. Seligman, citing work by Barbara Fredrickson, notes the evolutionary and life-enhancing prospects of positive emotions.[16] It turns out that positive emotions have benefits to the development and broadening of the intellectual, physical, and social dimensions of our lives. This also parallels Damasio's contention, mentioned earlier, that emotions are evolved homeostatic tools used for monitoring our degree of success as we interact with our environment. It has always seemed to me that Spinoza means to link a certain kind of open-ended efficacy with that of pleasure. Positive emotions not only reinforce successful action, but they also put one in a mode that is open to additional ways in which to enhance and expand any successful act. Positive psychology would call this the "outward spiral" effect of positive emotion.[17]

Emotions are, for the most part, passive for Spinoza, but in principle emotions can be either active or passive (E3P58). Active is the more positive term for Spinoza, and all active emotions are still rooted in pleasure and desire (E3P59). Spinoza describes being passive as having an emotion of which we are not the "adequate cause" and being active as having an emotion of which we are the "adequate cause" (E3Def.3). To be the adequate cause of our action is to have that action stem from "our nature" (E3Def.2), but in this respect Spinoza prefers to speak in terms of the *mind* being active. The expression of the mind being active is put in terms of having "adequate ideas." Emotions that are passive are correlated with inadequate or confused ideas, but if they were active they would be correlated with adequate or clear and distinct ideas.

I propose at this stage to leave off pursuing some of the technical aspects of explaining these terms further. We have said enough here to explain the main point as it applies to psychology—one that is not far from ordinary experience. To experience a pleasure may *move* me (notice that locution), but even though I am the one feeling it (notice that locution too), I seem not to be the one who is doing it; rather I am the one experiencing it. Even if I took some actions to bring that pleasure about, I am not, in this sense, the adequate cause of what I'm feeling.

The feelings are mine, to be sure. They belong to me and may have even been brought about by me, but that seems to leave open the question of when do we have just "me" rather than what belongs to or is produced in "me?" So far I seem *passive* with respect to the pleasures (and pains), as the locutions of the last sentences seem to testify. To get at that "me" alone would be in Spinoza's epistemology to say that I was acting from my nature, was the adequate cause of what I was doing, and thus that my actions stemmed from adequate ideas. When I am active and the adequate cause of what I am experiencing, the descriptions would tend to be less in terms of what I'm receiving (passive) and much more in terms of what I am *doing* (active).

For Spinoza, what I am doing when active is very much tied up with clear understanding. For me to understand clearly is not primarily a reference to a reflection upon my acts, such that when I consider them I know why I'm undertaking them. That may be part of it, but the idea of activity for Spinoza is more a function of *clarity in the act itself* than it is clarity in reflection upon the act. We might colloquially speak of this in terms of someone having a clear sense of purpose or of someone who "knows what she's doing." The person may have reflected often enough on how to do something, but now they are just doing it in a manner that clearly suggests control and mastery. A passive emotion may issue in the same or a similar behavior, but it is as if the person was drawn into or happened upon the action. If the meaningful life is the active life for Spinoza or the gratified life for positive psychology, it must thus be a life that draws us out. Passive emotions absorb the self; active emotions express it.

That "higher state of perfection" Spinoza speaks of when talking about pleasure is not simply a reference to what is currently the case about one's condition or actions, but also what is *becoming* the case in terms of the related advantages and opportunities yet to be exploited. We do not accurately describe the reality of a thing (remember "reality" = "perfection") by looking at simply what it is, but also by looking at the dispositions, propensities, implications, and opportunities that may be implicit in its ongoing activities. It seems quite reasonable to hypothesize about Spinoza, then, what is already present in positive psychology, namely, that positive emotions are a necessary foundation from which activity (or gratification) itself emerges. We are not born active for Spinoza (any more than we are by nature gratified). Indeed, we have to work at it, and most of mankind never achieves much activity in the Spinozistic sense. We are from birth, however, emotional responders to ourselves and our environment. The reinforcement and efficacy components of positive emotions would seem to be the natural soil within which activity (and gratification) proper for Spinoza would normally begin to flourish.

The active life is therefore given a much better chance of establishment and success where positive emotions are present. But the most interesting and important factor in the good life—that is, a life of significant gratification—is flow. As I understand positive psychology, activities that gratify us have high degrees of flow. While "consciousness and emotions are there to correct your trajectory; when what you are doing is seamlessly perfect, you don't need them."[18] Flow is that "seamlessly perfect" activity that describes the essence of gratification for positive psychology. The characteristics of flow—skill, concentration, deep involvement, timelessness, clarity, and the like—all suggest complete presence in the action. We do, rather than experience, and the more we are doing the less we are experiencing, if doing means we reflect less upon the experience. Moreover, because we are doing rather than monitoring, our focus is outward on the actions themselves and not inward on how we are feeling about them. Phenomenologically the movement in flow (activity) seems to be one of inward out, as opposed to an emotion (passive emotion) that seems to overtake us and thus move "outward" in. Flow is thus psychologically active; that is, it is not reflective upon a state of being and inner-directed, but engaged and outward directed. Spinoza speaks of acting from our own nature and being the cause, rather than the recipient, of what goes on in our behaviors. This is what it means to be "active" for Spinoza and is, I am suggesting, very much like what positive psychologists think of as flow.

It is, of course, somewhat anachronistic to apply "flow" to Spinoza, but from what I have been arguing, the basic components of flow and gratification do apply to what Spinoza means by activity. The case for this is inferential, but I believe plausible nonetheless, and I believe clarity is probably the key by which to make the connection. Consider what Spinoza says in his "general definition of emotions" given later in E3:

> The emotion called a passive experience is a confused idea whereby the mind affirms a greater or less force of existence of its body, or part of its body, than was previously the case, and by the occurrence of which the mind is determined to think of one thing rather than another.

Since passive emotions are confused ideas, we are active to the extent that our ideas are clear and distinct. In the case of positive emotions and activity, both would involve a greater "force of existence." But Spinoza seems to believe that without adequate ideas, we are likely to be "tossed about like the waves of the sea" (E3P59Schol.), however positive our emotions may be. With adequate ideas, however, we will apparently know what we are doing, how we are doing it, and why we are doing it. This clarity of focus suggests a certain self-directedness that is consistent with flow.

When I am fully absorbed in writing this chapter I'm paying little attention to how I feel and am more involved in expressing the connections between Spinoza and positive psychology or in clarifying Spinoza's conception of activity. If things are going particularly well, then I am clear not only about what I want to say, but how I want to say it. My actions seem to usher forth from within me without hesitation, doubt, or reflection. These actions seem wholly mine. It is here that we need to bring in another term from Spinoza's conception of activity that is central to his project and which may be applicable to an understanding of flow, and that is Spinoza's notion of freedom. This is a broad term that will occupy us for the remaining chapters. Nevertheless, it is appropriate that we introduce it here.

In a way, the point of Spinoza's ethics is not dissimilar to the recommendations of positive psychologists, namely, to take control of one's life by being less a victim of one's attitudes, moods, and emotions and to utilize those components of one's psychology and character that can lead to genuine gratification. It does not strain our language to say that should one reach "authentic happiness" one would be, in a very real way, free. Freedom is the point of parts four and five of Spinoza's *Ethics*, and Spinoza is referring primarily to a concept of freedom that is personal and psychological, that is, one that concerns how one conducts one's life rather than with a political or social notion of freedom. We know this because the enemy for Spinoza is bondage, which he claims is "man's lack of power to control and check the emotions" (E4Preface). So freedom will have something to do with self-direction and independence and the like. There is just one little problem we need to discuss first to get our discussion underway.

Power, Perfection, and Free Will

"Self-governance," "self-directedness," or "autonomy" in many philosophers of the liberal or Enlightenment era incorporate the idea of acting on decisions that are made by us through some process of reflection, critical examination, and self-directed rational deliberation. We think of such actions as essentially the product of our own wills rather than someone else's or some other factor outside of us. Thus, for example, we might think of how autonomous one is as a function of how authentically self-directed someone may be. Spinoza has no language of "autonomy" and not much use for terms such as "self-governance" or "self-direction." Rather, Spinoza, as we have seen, tends to use the language of activity and passivity (*agree* and *pati*). The problem with Spinoza, however, is that he wants to talk about freedom in an unfree universe! "Self-governance," "autonomy," and "self-direction" all seem to be terms that presuppose something like free will. But free will is precisely what Spinoza denies:

> In the mind there is no absolute, or free, will. The mind is determined to this or that volition by a cause, which is likewise determined by another cause, and this again by another, and so ad infinitum. (E2P48)

Spinoza's denial of free will is a function of his denial of any separation between the will and the intellect (E2P49Cor.). We tend to think of our ideas as one thing and our will as another, but it is not just that they go together for Spinoza, but rather that they are one and the same thing for him. We do not, therefore—as in a traditional understanding—first think about something and then freely will to put it in action or not. Rather, our ideas have within them their own powers to move us.

How that works will be the object of some of the discussion below. For the moment it is enough to simply note Spinoza's belief in the inherent motive power of ideas and to realize that Spinoza is not out to argue that freedom is impossible, but quite the contrary: Spinoza wants to distinguish free from unfree acts, just as do traditional free will doctrines. As it turns out, what promotes freedom is also what promotes well-being and is tied to activity. But seeing that is some way down the road. Let's first begin with our basic concepts of activity and passivity as they apply here. These terms are defined early on in the third book of Spinoza's *Ethics*:

> I say that we are active when something takes place, in us or externally to us, of which we are the adequate cause; that is, ... when from our nature there follows in us or externally to us something which can be clearly and distinctly understood through our nature alone. On the other hand, I say that we are passive when something takes place in us, or flows from our nature, of which we are only the partial cause. (E3Def.2)

Just preceding this, Spinoza gives us his definition of adequate and inadequate cause:

> I call that an adequate cause whose effect can be clearly and distinctly perceived through the said cause. I call that an inadequate or partial cause whose effect cannot be understood through the said cause alone. (E3Def.1)

For our purposes, what is important here is the connection Spinoza makes between these definitions and the "emotions" or affects that move us. This is important because the idea of freedom (and thus activity) is very much connected to the emotions for Spinoza. Typically, being governed by one's emotions is not a sign of "activity." Yet given Spinoza's somewhat specialized understanding of "emotion" we need to follow his definitions closely because there are exceptions. In the end, as we shall now start to see, he does not deviate that much from the tradition of seeing that emotions can be an impediment to "activity."

> By emotions (*affectus*) I understand the affections of the body by which the body's power of activity is increased or diminished, assisted or checked, together with the ideas of these affections.
>
> Thus if we can be the adequate cause of one of these affections, then by emotion I understand activity, otherwise passivity. (E3Def.3)

Spinoza's famous doctrine of parallelism, which holds that mind and body have corresponding but distinct descriptions for all events, indicates that we must pay some attention to both sides of the equation.[19] Hence he tells us, "the more the mind has inadequate ideas, the more it is subject to passive states; and, on the other hand, it is the more active in proportion as it has a greater number of adequate ideas" (E3P1Cor.). In these descriptions or definitions we see that activity has both a mental and physical dimension. The two are related through the concept of *conatus* and finally appetite. As we noted briefly at the beginning of the chapter, *conatus* is a kind of persistence or endeavoring true of both mind and body (E3P7). *Conatus* is thereby expressed through our essence, which turns out to be appetite. To expand a bit the passage we saw earlier:

> When this conatus is related to the mind alone, it is called Will; when it is related to mind and body together, it is called Appetite, which is therefore nothing else but man's essence (*ipsa hominis essentia*), from the nature of which there necessarily follow those things that tend to his preservation, and which man is thus determined to perform. Further, there is no difference between appetite and Desire except that desire is usually related to men in so far as they are conscious of their appetite. (E3P9Schol.)

The endeavor of mind and body exerting itself through and into the world is the base from which we can describe what we do as being either essentially active or passive. Heightened exertion is not, however, equivalent to activity, as we are reminded from the passage we saw earlier from E3P11Schol. (e.g., "I shall understand by pleasure 'the passive transition of the mind to a state of greater perfection,' and by pain 'the passive transition of the mind to a state of less perfection'"). As we have already seen, "perfection" and "reality" do, however, mean the same thing for Spinoza (E2Def.6). In general, then, activity is better than passivity because it carries with it more "reality." How this might look in actual practice we shall discuss later, but we can begin by noting the following:

> By *virtue* and *power* I mean the same thing; that is (E3P7),[20] virtue, insofar as it is related to man, is man's very essence, or nature, insofar as he has power to bring about that which can be understood solely through the laws of his own nature. (E4Def.8)

We are passive to the extent to which we need to explain our actions by what is "outside" of us. Of course, we can never attain complete activity according to Spinoza (E4P4), so the issue of passivity and activity is a relative one. But given that general caveat, we can move forward in discussing activity, passivity, freedom, and bondage.[21]

The key to Spinoza on the issues that concern us here, then, is provided in the opening line of the Preface to Part IV of the *Ethica*: "I assign the term 'bondage' (*servitutem*) to man's lack of power to control and check the emotions (*affectibus*)." Our passivity or bondage is a function of the degree to which we lack adequate ideas (E5P3), and the more adequate our ideas the more active and free we become (E5P10 & Schol.; E5P40). Our adequate ideas as modes of reason turn out to be a way of controlling our passive emotions (E5P7), which put us into bondage, and in the scholium to E5P20, for example, we get a brief summary account of how the mind might control the passive emotions so that we are able to move towards more freedom and activity. We can add to this the value component by noting that, "our active emotions, that is, those desires that are defined by man's power, that is, by reason, are always good; the other desires can be either good or evil" (E4App.#3). This statement shows both that there can be active emotions and that passive ones are not necessarily bad, though active ones are always good.

To the uninitiated, unpacking a paragraph like the foregoing one on bondage and freedom seems a necessity. To the initiated, doing so is nothing less than daunting! A full unpacking would require a survey of almost the whole of the secondary literature on Spinoza, since this topic is so fundamental to his *Ethics*.[22] Short of that, perhaps a few (hopefully salient) observations are in order here (more will follow in chapter 4). In general, I would like to borrow a metaphor from economics as a guide. Economists will sometimes speak of "internalizing the externalities" when referring to problems of market failure. For them, if costs are distributed widely but benefits captured by a few, the incentive to manage costs is weakened and inefficiencies result. That is, if one can get other people to bear the burden of the costs of one's actions, but one reaps most of the benefits (e.g., get a lot of people to pay for one's education), then one will have less of an incentive to economize on costs.

The corrective to this is to get the costs to be carried by those who will be reaping the benefits—to internalize the externality.

Now it is not costs and benefits that concern us, but the phraseology of internalizing what is external. For Spinoza, to be active is to be the source of our own actions and not to be impelled by forces external to us. We will always be impelled by some force in this system, but if what we are impelled by stems from us rather than something outside of us, we are active and free. In this case, our endeavors are internal when they "follow from the necessity of our nature" which means that we are the adequate cause of them. What we generally do not want is to be impelled by what is external to us, that is, by what does not follow from our nature alone and of which we are the partial cause. What is outside of us is what we do not understand, so if we do understand something it could be said that we have internalized it.

What may seem puzzling at first is to think of our emotions as being "external" to us. This is not, however, so strange as first appearances might suggest, because we are accustomed to speaking of being "taken over" by our emotions, as if they *were* outside of us in some way (see E4P20Schol.). In Spinoza, since appetite is our essence, and mind and body are in tandem in any appetite (by definition), our appetites only become our own, so to speak, when we are clear about what they are, what has given rise to them, and how they are functioning in the current situation. That is to say, we can be the "adequate cause" of what we do (our "effects") only if we are clear about the sources of our actions and their impact upon the environment in which they are undertaken. If we do not understand what we are doing, or do so only partially and inadequately, then it seems perfectly plausible to suggest that we are being moved by forces that are in some way not us—however much those forces may be located within our own bodies. For whether I have a pain that is causing me to squirm in my chair because I am sitting on something I do not see, or because there is some neural malfunction inside my body seems to have little to do with *me* being the cause of my squirming. If, however, I squirm because I understand that my discomfort is being caused by something sticking through the bottom of the chair and I will be able to displace it by my squirming in such a way that I am no longer affected, then my squirming would seem to be an action of mine rather than something I am noticing about myself.

Emotions are a certain type of reaction to stimuli given to us physically by our environment. That environment could be "inside" of us or "outside." As we saw earlier, there can be active emotions. For an emotion to be active, it would have to stem from the presence of adequate ideas (E3P58), but this is not likely to be our ordinary state (E4P4–6). Passive emotions are far and away the most common ones, and are seen by Spinoza as being in a significant way "external" to us (E4P5). The project of freedom, then, is one of internalizing our emotions; that is, making them a function of adequate rather than inadequate ideas. We succeed in this project either by checking or by replacing our passive emotions with more active ones (E4P7,14,59,61), thus harnessing their power in ways that are clear to us. But we should not expect passive emotions to disappear, and they are quite capable of ruling us entirely (E4P6). That is why freedom is an achievement that draws us out of our ordinary state of passivity. Our very finitude and the limited character of our power relative to the universe around us not only indicates why our freedom can never be complete, but also how difficult and fragile is its achievement.

Already we saw in the foregoing description of Spinoza's concept of activity and freedom some parallels to ideas of activity as we described them earlier. Activity is a kind of self-causation which links up nicely with notions of self-determination, self-government, autonomy, self-directedness, and agency. We are the authors and source of our actions, because they are caused by our nature. Furthermore, with activity being a function of adequate ideas, we are reminded of the requirements of rationality built into many notions of activity, since the adequacy of our ideas is more often than not provided by reason.[23] To have a clear understanding about our motivations and what we are doing would certainly seem to parallel some of the requirements for considered rationality common in many notions of activity. Indeed, the call for activity over passivity rules out impulsive or passionate behavior. These terms we have been discussing deal more with agency and self-perfectionist forms of activity than what we shall call "morality" in the next chapter. The point at this stage, however, is to suggest that Spinoza's philosophy, however different in structure it may be from other forms, where terms like "choice" or "autonomy" are more explicitly mentioned, nevertheless accords a central place for freedom. That is, Spinoza draws an important distinction between self-governed and self-directed conduct on the one hand, and the sort where one is pushed and pulled by forces outside of oneself on the other.

One may still want to claim that there must be "free will" somewhere in the picture for one to put oneself in a position to achieve freedom as Spinoza defines it. Otherwise, it will be the case that the free and unfree are in their respective states through no acts of their own. Of course, an "act of one's own" *just is* being active for Spinoza, so the question really is not about whether we have a choice to be free, but whether the movement from passivity to activity is something we have any choice about. For if we are already "free" in Spinoza's sense, the issue of whether we are so "by choice" is something of a purely academic exercise. Presumably what we want to know is whether we can do anything to bring ourselves from a state of passivity to activity. The glib Spinozistic answer to this question is "of course!" Insofar as we were once passive and are now active, each of us who has made this transition has, by definition, "acted on one's own;" for that is what it means to be active.

The less glib answer—the one I shall adopt here—is really not so very different. This "answer" is to avoid taking on the question directly and simply going about our business of noting the differences between activity and passivity and the ways in which one may understand one's actions in either state. If we do that, and one understands the ideas and suggestions related to the difference, then perhaps the power of ideas alone is enough to move one in the right direction.[24] It would be, in other words, no different from what happens when one reads a book on how to improve one's life. One either follows the advice or not. Either way, the process looks suspiciously like the process of self-improvement people have used throughout history; and if that is so, the question of whether there is something called "free will" that made the transition possible becomes increasingly academic and sterile.

Chapter Three

The Ethics of Activity

"A Man of thorow *Good-Breeding*, whatever else he be, is incapable of doing a rude or brutal Action. He never *deliberates* in this case, or considers of the matter by prudential Rules of Self-Interest and Advantage. He acts from his Nature, in a manner necessarily, and without Reflection: and if he did not, it were impossible for him to answer his Character, or be found that truly well-bred Man, on every occasion."

—*Shaftesbury*, "An Essay on the Freedom of Wit and Humour"

Spinoza's ethics is not easily described. Don Garrett tells us "Spinoza is both a consequentialist and a virtue ethicist."[1] In a connected vein, Lee C. Rice[2] claims we should describe Spinoza as a "classical" moralist. The essential element in Spinoza's classicism being described by Rice as follows:

> [Spinoza's] ethical theory is classical in structure. It is not, like contemporary metaethical theories, an account of normative predication and the function of normative discourse in language, but rather a first-order normative theory which purports to outline and argue the prospects for human well-being (Aristotle's *eudaimonia*, Spinoza's *beatitudo*) in a system of nature viewed as largely amoral.[3]

Another way of putting the point about it being classical in nature is to say that Spinoza's ethics is not like most modern ethical theories in being centrally concerned with questions of obligation, duty, or one's social roles with respect to others. Instead, the approach would be typically described as one focused on the good, but for reasons somewhat peculiar to Spinoza,[4] it is best to think in terms of an orientation towards well-being or "perfection." It is thus consequentialist in looking to the effects of action upon well-being. It is virtue oriented in that well-being resides mostly in developed qualities of character and mind. It is the combination of these two elements that jointly give rise to what I call Spinoza's ethics of immanence. An ethics of immanence is one whose object is essentially the self-perfection or self-empowerment of the individual. Willi Goetschel offers an excellent summary of the basis of this approach to ethics:

> Spinoza's *Ethics* can in this way be understood as a philosophy of self-empowerment in the precise meaning of the term. ... Although Spinoza redefines the concept of autonomy and freedom in a way that has led to the dismissal of his philosophy as reductive and determinist, his reformulation of human freedom and autonomy in terms of self-determination and self-preservation, understood as self-realization, breaks new ground for a dynamic conception of individuality that takes the psychosomatic constitution of human nature as the basis for the individual's open-ended potential for self-realization.[5]

As we move forward in this and the next chapter, we hope to see more clearly just what self-determination and self-preservation amount to, in addition to exploring the meaning of open-ended self-realization. For now, one can see that with Spinoza talk about "ethics" will have a distinctly different flavor than such discussion usually exhibits.

In this regard, we would follow Lee C. Rice again who claims that we must, for Spinoza, draw a strong distinction between ethics on the one hand and morality on the other.[6] The citation by Rice above explains one reason for drawing this distinction, namely that morality concerns the application of such normative predicates as "right" or "wrong," "just" or "unjust," "virtuous" or "vicious," and the like, and not how to live a life. There is another reason, however, for drawing some such distinction,[7] and the simplest way of putting this point is to say that ethics concerns human activity, whereas morality concerns itself with either what is passive or with forms of passivity that would receive endorsement by reason were the action to spring from adequate ideas. In both cases, factors contributory to human well-being are the foundations for any descriptions of normative value, but something may contribute to human well-being which is not in itself active.

Spinoza indicates the difference between morality and ethics when he tells us that, "if men were born free, they would form no conception of good and evil so long as they were free" (E4P68). The meaning of this proposition is connected to the general thesis that nature acts neither for nor against us (and thus contains no good or evil in itself), but follows its own inexorable laws. Within this framework the proposition is a way of saying that good and evil, as terms of ordinary moral discourse, reflect the inadequacy of our ideas to understand the inexorable course of nature. As we saw in the last chapter, we are passive when our ideas are inadequate. In a passive condition, we are moved by things "outside" of ourselves which we do not fully understand or know how to internalize within our own active conduct. We would under such conditions come to see things in the world as being either for (good) or against (evil) us. If, on the other hand, we had adequate ideas, we would know that nothing out there was in itself for or against us, that what is happening is the result of intelligible causes, and that we would be doing all that can be done, and only what could be done, to expand our power into that environment. We cannot suppose that the active person could do something differently, because that would be to suppose she could recognize the "correct" course but not undertake it. For Spinoza, will and intellect are the same (E2P49Cor.), so understanding what to do is already to be doing it. Acts of prior deliberation about what to do and which course or action is better or worse are to some extent expressions of mental confusion. In the discussion of activity in the preceding chapter we saw the foundations for this claim. To know what is right is not to then do the right but to *be doing* the right, for the knowing and the doing would be simultaneous and coextensive, with no reflections on "good" or "evil."

That the right action is the only *action* does have some resemblance to Kant's claim that acting from duty is described both as autonomy and the only thing a rational being could choose to do. In Spinoza's case, however, one does not first become rational and then will that rationality into practice. Rather, rationality is expressed. It is not a detached conclusion waiting to be engaged with the world, but the activity of engagement itself.[8] The notion that we cannot have adequate ideas about our actions which are waiting to be engaged explains why Spinoza is more comfortable with an exemplar model of ethics than ones which articulate principles or rules of conduct, themselves the product of discursive rationality (E5P10Schol.). An exemplar, being a model of an agent in action, is closer to the very doing of the actions than is a set of principles to be followed.[9]

The psychological disposition we are exploring here is not unknown to ethical theory and might be suggested in the difference between the attitude of the so-called "rescuers" during the Second World War and that of most other people at that time (or us imagining ourselves back then). Everyone would agree that the Jew pursued by the Nazi is being victimized. The rescuer (the one who hid or helped the Jew), however, offered help and did that without a sense that there was anything else to be done under the circumstances. One would expect that most others, by contrast, are likely to have wondered about the extent and meaning of their "obligation" to provide aid under such circumstances, whether their own interests outweighed that of the endangered Jews, whether the risk to others was a stronger obligation than the contemplated aid, and the like. Understood in this way, morality, as it is normally conceived and practiced, is a sign of our passivity and uncertainty, and Spinoza tells us as much in E5P10Schol.—"Therefore the best course we can adopt, as long as we do not have perfect knowledge of our emotions, is to conceive a right method of living, or fixed rules of life. ..."

Spinoza is quick to point out in the scholium to E4P68 (the one previously mentioned where we can form no conception of good or evil if born free) that we are definitely not born free, or ever achieve it fully. We are limited creatures of very finite dimensions and abilities and often subject to forces well beyond our control. The whole proposition (E4P68 + scholium) is therefore illustrative, not descriptive. We see from it just how distinctive human freedom is from the forces that usually govern us. We should also see why it is likely that morality will be a necessary feature of human life; for given our passivity, the same reasons just articulated for saying that morality is passive are the ones which explain its necessary presence in human life—we will need various aids in overcoming our passivity. In this connection I would want to claim that morality, while passive in itself, is nevertheless the bridge to the active and may possess active elements under some circumstances. But to see this point, we need to understand passivity a bit more as it applies to ethics.

Spinoza's ethics takes place on three levels (pleasure and pain, the socially useful, and self-perfection or "blessedness"). We have elsewhere described these levels as "three levels of the good."[10] The first level is simply the level of individual pleasure and pain (E3P39Schol.). Here the individual is considered more or less in isolation, with pleasure and pain either encouraging or discouraging the individual's endeavors. Of course, as Spinoza points out (E3P11Schol., P28–29) and as we discussed in the last chapter, the basis for the next level is grounded in the first. The second level could be called the socially useful, which originates in pleasure and pain transformed into the various emotions that ground our relationships with one another and ourselves (E3P30,ff). In a social setting Spinoza uses the word "useful" (*utile*) and tends to judge the "well being" of social orders in terms of what is useful to them[11] (TTP XVI, XX; TP II 18–20, V 1–3). In any case, the idea here is complicated. The "useful" encompasses custom, law, authority, and culture as they affect us in various ways, as well as utility more ordinarily understood as what benefits us. These social settings and forces are among the things that compel us. We are passive with respect to them, but properly ordered they would be both necessary and beneficial and will tend to benefit most of us collectively overall. Consider,

> Conduct that brings about harmony is that which is related to justice, equity, and honorable dealing. For apart from resenting injustice and unfairness, men also resent what is held to be base, or contempt for the accepted customs of the state. But for winning their love the most important factors are those connected to religion and piety. (E4App.#15)

Here we see affective elements dominating the moral enterprise considered from a social point of view.

Spinoza anticipates here, at least logically, the more systematic accounts of morality developed by thinkers such as Hume and Smith. If morality were passive, it would then become a matter of understanding just how the affections can give rise to moral norms and conduct. The working out of the mechanisms for this approach to ethics is a way of seeing how the "sentiments" can fashion our moral universe—a project that extends from Hutcheson through Smith and beyond. Reason, for the most part, is not the basis of morality. We interact with each other affectively, and the multiplicity and diversity of those interactions across the society get generalized and codified into norms of conduct and standards for according merit and demerit, propriety and impropriety, to actions and individuals. There is virtually no fundamental questioning or understanding of these collective norms on the part of the vast majority of individuals who act under them and according to them. Moreover, it is evident that strong sentiments for their adherence and against their violation are attached to the moral sentiments themselves, serving to reinforce the norms as springs of actual conduct.

In the *Ethics* the passages that provide the transition from morality passively considered to a more active form are found primarily from E4P30 to E4P37, though E4P40 sums up the point most succinctly. Morality might be passive in its origin and general functioning, but it can also accord with what is active and be a form of conduct an active person would undertake or presuppose. In this part of the *Ethics*, the language is mixed, alternating between the active and the passive. Perhaps the following passage from E4P37Schol.2 best indicates the general passivity that pervades morality and its possible connection to activity.

> Every man judges what is good and what is bad, and has regard for his own advantage according to his own way of thinking ... and seeks revenge ... and endeavors to preserve what he loves and to destroy what he hates. ... Now if men lived by the guidance of reason, every man would possess this right of his ... without any harm to another. But since men are subject to emotions ... which far surpass the power or virtue of men ... they are therefore often pulled in different directions ... and are contrary to one another ... while needing each other's help. ... It is necessary ... to create a feeling of mutual confidence that they will refrain from any action that may be harmful to another. The way to bring this about (that men who are necessarily subject to passive emotions ... and are inconstant and variable ... should establish a mutual confidence and

should trust one another) is obvious. ... It was demonstrated that no emotion can be checked except by a stronger emotion contrary to the emotion which is to be checked, and that every man refrains from inflicting injury through fear of greater injury. On these terms, then, society can be established ... if it has the power to prescribe common rules of behavior and to pass laws to enforce them, not by reason, which is incapable of checking the emotions ... but by threats.

That human beings should unite and can live in harmony to their mutual advantage according to "common rules" is something suggested by reason, but also something that needs to be put in place among beings *not* guided by reason. Consequently, however important the common rules may be to a rational consideration of social interaction, the passage shows that they are clearly not *e*ffective unless they are first affective. The only potentially misleading feature of this passage is its emphasis on threats. While the power to enforce must be somewhere at the foundations of the social system, it is more accurate to say of Spinoza that he favors inducements and incentives over threats and fear as a mechanism for social control and unity.[12]

As I have suggested, the affective turn in ethics so prominent in the 18th century may be a recognition of the truths about human beings just mentioned. The sophisticated sympathetic mechanisms of morality described by Hume and Smith, which indicate the affective qualities of moral norms in practice, are valuable extensions to the Spinozistic project. In the end, however, we are still dealing largely with passivity from a Spinozistic point of view. The recognition of this was certainly, if only tacitly, a motivation for Kant to find some role for reason within this sort of outlook on ethics. Like Kant, Spinoza might be willing to say that the rational man would will the principles for himself, even while others may follow them for other reasons. Unlike Kant, actions not taken in a state of activity are not necessarily devoid of moral content. And as we have seen, one's freedom for Spinoza does not consist in a grasp of generalized principles, but almost the reverse—in the particular form of one's endeavoring. To see this, let's take a specific example, in this case of an automobile mechanic.

A person merely knowledgeable about auto mechanics is not thereby free for Spinoza simply in his knowledge of the working of cars, and certainly not in his knowledge of the *theory* of auto mechanics.

It is generally more correct to say that one is free or active to the extent one has both understood and applied those principles in the past, and most free when one is endeavoring with them in the present. It is the extension of the general into the particular that gives us activity—not simply the possession of general knowledge. So a person facing the breakdown of a car by using knowledge to repair the disruptive defect is more active than the person of similar knowledge who merely argues well about what ought to be done or who remains in the car for fear of soiling his hands. We cannot make the transition to the required sort of activity without the general principles reason provides, but those principles are not freedom in themselves. So we make the move to the third and highest level of the good through the universal, but universal principles do not describe it. That third level, which Spinoza calls "blessedness" in some contexts, but which for us here is "activity," is a form of personal self-perfection through the adequacy of our ideas. We need to explore briefly its distinctiveness from passivity, leaving aside for later the many dimensions of piety and the intellectual love of God Spinoza also discusses in connection with "blessedness." [13]

If we start with ideas, we have already noted that they carry with them their own forms of perfection, which means their own power of affirmation and negation (E2P49Schol.). A powerful and clear idea is presumably one that leads us on to others. A confused and weak one is one that leaves us unable to give a precise account of the idea or leaves us without an ability to integrate it well with other ideas. If then our essence is appetite, which unites the conatus of our ideas with that of our body (pleasure and pain), then ideas about action will only tend to withdraw us from the world if they are in some way defective, inadequate, confused, or painful. Effective, adequate, and pleasurable ideas would only encourage more of the same. The free person thinks of death least of all things. The life of the mind, assuming in this case that the mind's object is action, will not issue in quietistic withdrawal but in ever more enthusiastic action.

In light of this last point, we should note that what is missing from our account so far is a certain distinctive *tone* to the argument that comes from Spinoza's use of terms like power, virtue, and reality. First of all, we might remind ourselves of Spinoza's parallelism as mentioned in

E3P11: "whatsoever increases or diminishes, assists or checks, the power of activity of our body, the idea of the said thing increases or diminishes, assists or checks the power of thought of our mind." This proposition is followed by his definitions of pleasure and pain already mentioned in chapter two. With this in mind perhaps the transition from what we have been saying, and what is unique to Spinoza's ethics, is conveyed in the following passage:

> [T]rue virtue is nothing other than to live by the guidance of reason, and so weakness consists solely in this, that a man suffers himself to be led by things external to himself and is determined by them to act in a way required by the general state of external circumstances, not by his own nature considered only in itself. (E4P37Schol.)

Recall that for Spinoza power and virtue are the same, so by this account reason gives us power and weakness is a function of inadequate ideas about ourselves and the environment in which we act. Recall also that power and perfection are the same and that pleasure increases our perfection, while pain diminishes it. From this we can see that virtue and conatus are intimately joined in a way that makes "activity" significantly more connected with successful self-extension and efficacy than what might be found in typical responsibility-based conceptions of activity. Consider in this regard the following:

> The more every man endeavors and is able to seek his own advantage, that is, to preserve his own being, the more he is endowed with virtue. On the other hand, insofar as he neglects to preserve what is to his advantage, that is, his own being, to that extent he is weak. (E4P20)

Furthermore,

> To act in absolute conformity with virtue is nothing else in us but to act, to live, to preserve one's own being (these three mean the same) under the guidance of reason, on the basis of seeking one's own advantage. (E4P24)

With these passages in mind, we can reaffirm that one's "activity" for Spinoza can be measured by one's success in extending one's power in, through, and over one's environment. The approach is thus not one of determining the degree of activity by measuring the extent to which one lives up to criteria of responsible conduct. Virtually the reverse of this approach is true in Spinoza: successful living just *is* the standard of activity for Spinoza, and our notions of what it might mean to be responsible for what we do might be better understood in light of success than in light of some prior conceptions of responsibility. But however responsibility is understood, it is not meant to be understood by Spinoza apart from other people.

The propositions (35–40) which are literally central to Part IV of the *Ethics* and which I am claiming are transition propositions from knowledge and good at level two to level three, are essentially about internalizing the powers of others with oneself for effective flourishing for all. It is here that one might seek to develop a perfectionistic political interpretation of Spinoza, an interpretation we saw as mistaken, but not completely implausible. For my part, when Spinoza does talk about politics in these propositions, he drops away from reason and back to affection (e.g., E4P37Schol.2), so I believe the case only confirms what we said in chapter one.

In any case, it is clear that harmonious interaction with others accords with reason and it would be something "willed" by the active person. "There is no individual thing in the universe more advantageous to man than a man who lives by the guidance of reason" (E4P35 Cor.1). We are told this is so because these individuals "agree in nature" with us. We learn, then, that our power of action is most enhanced by the joint efforts of other human beings in a social setting where such individuals understand what they are doing. This is a form of cooperation where the parties involved are clear about what they are doing and their respective roles in the joint enterprise—in other words, they are active. We are less effective when we are at odds with one another, an increased possibility when we are passive (E4P34). For obviously if people are in conflict they are not engaged in accomplishing some mutually beneficial objective.

The recognition of the mutual "gains from trade" that the active person finds in others of like nature might be seen as the "dignity" component in Spinoza's theory of "autonomy." Other agents are inherently of value, because their value derives from their nature—that is, the value is *inherent* within them and recognized as such by others.

Or to put this another way, as active agents they are the adequate causes of their own conduct, and given that such people are of most value to us, that value is internalized within them and comes completely from them. The inherent character of value within active agency is just as true when speaking of the agent, because passivity can lead to internal conflict as well. But since most of us are passive most of the time, full activity tends to escape us. As a consequence, it would be unlikely that this sort of "dignity" can be the basis upon which to build a political philosophy, nor even much of a social ethics. For while the active agent will certainly endorse some of the general rules of ethics, those rules would have little meaning if they were dependent upon a predominance of active agents. Recognizing this, Kant makes a transcendental turn away from individuals found in experience in order to find the sort of autonomous rationality necessary, he believes, to ground inherent dignity. For Spinoza, the achievement of inherent value would be an increasing form of *immanent* self-perfection. But our nature as less than fully perfected beings is such that we always have some varying degrees of virtue with respect to each other.

Character Strengths and Virtues in Spinoza

Keeping in mind that part of our well being is connected to linking the good and meaningful lives mentioned in chapter two to activity and ethics, we take as our starting point in this subsection the character strengths and virtues as they have been identified by positive psychology. The six core moral virtues identified by positive psychology are as follows: wisdom and knowledge, courage, humanity, justice, temperance, and transcendence.[14] There are a number of subcategories of virtues that fall underneath each of these core virtues. Courage, for example, includes bravery, persistence, integrity, and vitality. Positive psychology believes that the six core virtues are ubiquitous across cultures and time. We shall not dispute this or the way in which positive psychology has catalogued the core virtues and their subcategories. But when asked to speculate on why these core virtues are ubiquitous, the answer is that their commonality derives from the fact that they have served us well in our development as human beings and thus have been selected for by a process of evolution.[15] For philosophers, this answer sends up a number of red flags, especially if we are linking virtues to morality. Nevertheless, insofar as we can speak of virtues in Spinoza, they would have value for Spinoza *precisely because* of their contribution to successful living. For Spinoza—for whom applying the idea of evolutionary selection, though completely anachronistic, would not be inconsistent with his views—these qualities of character would not be valuable because they are right, but right because they are valuable. They would enhance our power to deal successfully with our environment.[16] In this way Spinoza and positive psychology can be closely connected, because both would identify virtue with some form of successful living.

Yet it seems to me something of a profitless exercise to look through Spinoza for examples of the six core virtues and many of their subcategories and how each contributes to successful living. No doubt we can find all six there if we look, with some such as wisdom being obviously so. It is more what Spinoza *emphasizes* to which I wish to give some attention. Wisdom is one of those points of emphasis. Spinoza tells us explicitly that "it is of the first importance in life to perfect the intellect" (E4App.#4). This is hardly surprising given all we have said about the relationship between adequate ideas and activity. As we noted also, there is a tendency in interpreting Spinoza, brought on by Spinoza himself in the fifth book of the *Ethics*, to claim that the best life is the contemplative, even mystical, one. The intellectual love of God and blessedness are the stated goals of the fifth book, and Spinoza himself lived something of a reclusive life as a philosopher. Though I am not convinced that the contemplative life is the only best life implied by Spinozism, I shall be arguing below that some form of intellectualism is indeed needed.

Yet whatever the "correct" interpretation of Spinoza, it is clear that what he says is not at all inconsistent with a less intellectualist interpretation.

> [T]he man who is guided by reason, the final goal, that is, the highest Desire whereby he strives to control all the others, is that by which he is brought to an adequate conception of himself and of all the things that can fall within the scope of his understanding. (E4App.#4)

This sort of advice need not require one to be a philosopher or a monk. There are reasons to know ourselves and apply our intelligence in every aspect of our lives. The interpretative problem is much like the one in Aristotle of trying to reconcile the "contemplative" life with Aristotle's "second best" life of practical virtue. Aristotle's *phronimos* (person of practical wisdom) perhaps mitigates somewhat the starkness of the contrast, since he combines both wisdom and action. It is in that spirit that I read the foregoing passage from Spinoza as well. Spinoza is an advocate of practical wisdom.

If one continues further beyond wisdom at what else Spinoza might value as a virtue, what strikes one first is the positive nature of Spinoza's approach. Spinoza is not an idealist who thinks life can exist without problems, pain, or failure. But the overall direction of his normative theory is completely positive. He tell us, for example, that

> His [a person's] prime endeavor is to conceive things as they are in themselves and to remove obstacles to true knowledge, such as hatred, anger, envy, derision, pride, and similar emotions that we have noted. And so he endeavors, as far as he can, to do well and to be glad, as we have said. (E4P73Schol.)

In addition Spinoza says the following:

> Therefore he who aims solely from love of freedom to control his emotions and appetites will strive his best to familiarize himself with virtues and their causes and to fill his mind with the joy that arises from the true knowledge of them, while refraining from dwelling on men's faults and abusing mankind and deriving pleasure from a false show of freedom. (E5P10Schol.)

Perhaps most strikingly we have the following:

> Cheerfulness [*hilaritas*] (pleasure simultaneously related to mind and body) cannot be excessive; it is always good. On the other hand, melancholy is always bad. (E4P42)

Joy, gladness, and cheerfulness are key terms in these passages, emphasizing once again the positive aspects of Spinoza's philosophy.[17] But these passages not only reflect a positive conception of a virtuous state of being, but they begin to indicate as well patterns of conduct that reflect virtues other than wisdom. What is particularly striking about reading Spinoza is how much emphasis he places upon the core virtue of humanity. We can see the negative side of this in the passages above, for what is clearly destructive are those emotions and patterns of conduct that impede interpersonal conduct, such as the emotions listed in the first passage and the abuse and derision of the second passage.

It may seem strange at first, but Spinoza's emphasis upon the virtue of humanity is not an unconnected deviation from his push for power that is at the center of his theory. Spinoza is clear that "nothing is more advantageous to man than man" (E4P18Schol.).[18] Moreover, "men will still discover from experience that they can much more easily meet their needs by mutual help and can ward off ever-threatening perils only by joining forces" (E4P35Cor.2Schol.). We can thus say with assurance that "whatever is conducive to man's social organization, or causes men to live in harmony, is advantageous" (E4P40). Social cooperation turns out to be power enhancing to each of us as individuals and to the groups and societies to which we belong. Some emotions (e.g., hatred or pride) hinder us as individuals from effectively engaging in social cooperation. Other patterns of behavior (derision, abuse, envy) destroy the social bonds that may be present and are necessary for our own success. The spiteful, the envious, the small-minded, and the jealous are particularly grievous under Spinoza's philosophy. These negative emotions or patterns of conduct retard both the individual as well as the society around her.[19]

But the story is not simply a negative one. It is clear from reading Spinoza that we should revel in the success of others, for the benefits of that always redound to ourselves. Consequently, Spinoza emphasizes "justice, equity, and honorable dealing" and "piety" (E4App.#15) along with "generosity" (#17) "marriage" (#20) and "courtesy" (#25) when speaking positively of emotions or virtues. He particularly emphasizes "gratefulness" and "gratitude" (E4P71& Schol.) and "good faith" in our conduct with others (E4P72). A number of the core virtues and their subcategories are thus traversed in the virtues Spinoza does emphasize. We have mentioned humanity, but aspects of the core virtues of justice and transcendence are clearly incorporated as well. The "good life," then, is essentially social in nature for Spinoza, and the signature strengths we employ in gaining gratification would most always be engaged in the company of others. Though positive psychology seems to remain officially neutral between its core virtues, Spinoza's emphasis on wisdom and humanity reflect premises that are both descriptive and normative—namely, the principle of power, reality, or perfection in action and the view that our success even as seekers of wisdom remains integrally connected to our ability to cooperate with others. If these are not the emphases of positive psychology, they do not stand in contradiction to it either.

We must conclude this section by returning to a problem already alluded to. If virtue is connected to power, then virtue must be connected to activity. But most people most of the time are not active in Spinoza's sense, but passive. That would suggest there is little virtue to be found. But if virtue is so rare, then it would seem—by the opening pages of this chapter and what we have said about successful living—that mental health would be rare and unavailable to most people, or if not unavailable, at least an unlikely prospect. That in turn would seem to contradict a tenet of positive psychology that health is available to all, and actually contradicts Spinoza's idea that virtue is open to all. Furthermore, apart from being too demanding a doctrine, the *positive* role of "passivity" would seem to be lost entirely, at least in Spinoza's case. For virtue would seem always to be only active and thus good, and passivity always be non-virtuous or bad, and thus to be avoided. The bipolar character of virtue or unvirtue (vice) would seem to leave no middle ground. Is Spinoza so completely void of a middle ground between activity on the one hand and passivity on the other? Is there a form of passivity in Spinoza that is "positive" and yet not fully active? And is this a form of "passivity" one that exists in the realm of virtue and not merely in the realm of positive emotion?

I think there is a realm of "passivity" in Spinoza that is still very positive yet may not require full freedom or activity on the part of the agent to realize. That Spinoza is willing to contemplate a "middle way" is indicated throughout book four of the *Ethics*. At certain points, for example, he tells us that humility, repentance, hope, and fear are not virtues (E4P47, 53, 54). At the same time, he is willing to say that "as men seldom live according to the dictates of reason, these two emotions, humility and repentance, and also hope and fear, bring more advantage than harm" (E4P54Schol.). He follows that sentence by saying that "in fact those who are subject to these emotions can be far more readily induced than others to live by the guidance of reason in the end, that is, to become free men and enjoy the life of the blessed." Obviously Spinoza is open to the benefits of certain dispositions even if they are not fully active and rational. One reason is their utility.

But another reason is also given, and it is one hinted at in the foregoing citation, namely the distinction between acting in accordance with reason and acting out of reason. As we have already noted on a number of previous occasions, actions in accordance with reason may be passive, but they are still the sorts of things in which one guided by reason alone would engage. As it turns out, most of the virtues of social cooperation can be understood in both ways. This is because they would be recommended to reason in their own right, but also because they can serve as a "model of human nature" (E4Preface) that can be adopted by those not yet fully active who can be induced to the social harmony that benefits us all. Indeed, passive or not, we must do this.

> Therefore, in order that men may live in harmony and help one another, it is necessary for them to give up their natural right and to create a feeling of mutual confidence that they will refrain from any action that may be harmful to another. The way to bring this about (that men who are necessarily subject to passive emotions ... and are inconstant and variable ... should establish a mutual confidence and should trust one another) is obvious. ... (E4P37Schol.2)

Of course, all this leads us into Spinoza's social and political philosophy which we touched upon already in chapter one. But the point that concerns us here can now be stated simply enough: there are surrogates for pure activity that are often expressed through the customs, mores, laws, and habits of people living in society. These are both useful and "according to reason." They are also available to all and can be followed by all. When it comes to virtue, for Spinoza, we are thus not sentenced to attain either failure or complete success with nothing in between qualifying as virtue to aid us. Quite the opposite. With the basis of what accords with reason, we have a strong foundation from which to act by reason.

Positive psychology's problem would seem to be the opposite of Spinoza's. In its cataloguing of virtues and character strengths, it looks for statistical regularity and universality. Yet although this way of deriving virtues may be enough to get us the good life, can it do what is necessary to move us to the meaningful life? The question is, can a meaningful life be obtained through practices alone or does there need to be some account or understanding of it? A meaningful life would seem to depend on some understanding about why the virtues are virtues and why there may be a need for prioritizing some of them over others, even at a generic level. In this respect, the approach affects the theory. The meaningful life for the positive psychologist may be as much a function of the procedural nature of its approach to virtue as Spinoza's emphasis on adequate ideation is to his view of the final stage needed for a "full" life. In other words, the positive psychologist gives no account of why virtues are virtues. Spinoza, by contrast, has a further account to give which will affect what he means by "meaningful life," if he were to use such terms. We turn to this issue in the next chapter. For the moment, let's conclude with some statement of what ethics is for Spinoza.

Ethics and Activity

On the basis of the foregoing, I want to suggest that there is very little "ethics" in the *Ethics*, at least as we normally understand "ethics." As we have noted, Spinoza says little about our obligations and more about our self-perfection. In addition, it seems that we can say that modes of moral thinking are not likely to be the first or necessarily a primary consideration for Spinoza when conceptualizing effective approaches to human interaction. If moral modes of reasoning are attempts to locate cases under their appropriate normative rules, roles, or obligations, then this may be a good deal less optimal than the recommendation to simply secure mutual agreement. In other words, rather than looking to a rule or principle that might cover what one should do in a given case, one decides what to do on the basis of what the parties involved find mutually advantageous. On this reading, individuals interact largely as individuals and not as repositories of familial, community, or other special obligations that they bring to a situation. There would be, of course, limiting conditions to any mutual agreements that are given by the basic principles of social order that get established in the formation of political society. But active people know that harming others or breaking promises are not conducive to cooperation and therefore not conducive to the effective enhancement of their joint power. So although their actions might be "universalizable" in some way, these active individuals are not looking for principles to guide them in what they do or in how best to exhibit respect for one another, but rather in discovering specific ways in which their separate powers might be jointly exercised to achieve maximum effectiveness. The process is a great deal more tailored to the capacities and circumstances of the actors involved, than is action in accordance with universalized normative rules.

Though Spinoza's conclusions are often different from other philosophical conclusions traditionally understood, he is not cut off from the tradition completely. As it turns out, for example, the degree to which one is free is the degree to which one is virtuous for Spinoza—much as any traditional ethicist might have said. But, of course, when one begins to explore the meaning of some of Spinoza's concepts, one may discover a number of non-traditional ideas. What, then, does Spinoza mean by virtue? We saw in the previous chapter that he is very direct: "by virtue and power I mean the same thing" (E4Def.8). Of course, as one might expect, there's a bit more: "that is ... virtue, insofar as it is related to man, is man's very essence, or nature, insofar as he has power to bring about that which can be understood solely through the laws of his own nature." Perhaps that description only confuses rather than clarifies, but it should be evident that Spinoza is referring to what we mentioned earlier, namely, actions which stem from us, that is, in which we are the "adequate cause" and that stem from our "nature."

The concepts that are linked together are thus the following: virtue→power→activity→adequate ideas→reason→perfection→reality = freedom. It matters little which concept you start with; they all refer back to each other. But the main idea I want to emphasize here, since dealing with all these concepts adequately would be much too extended a task, is that freedom, virtue, and what might be called "self-determination" are very much equated in Spinoza.[20] This brings us back to the simple and direct, yet surprisingly complete, description of virtue found in Spinoza.

> [T]rue virtue is nothing other than to live by the guidance of reason, and so weakness consists solely in this, that a man suffers himself to be led by things external to himself and is determined by them to act in a way required by the general state of external circumstances, not by his own nature considered only in itself. (E4P37Schol.1)

One interpretation that might be given to this passage is an intellectualist gloss. The contemplative life is the life of true virtue. Given what Spinoza says in the fifth book of the *Ethics* and in his *Treatise on the Emendation of the Intellect*, this interpretation is not implausible. Nonetheless, I intend to interpret the use of "reason" in the foregoing passage in a way that is at least partly reflected in our automobile example; that is, reason is understanding one's own actions and the circumstances in which one is undertaking those actions. Clearly, knowledge is power for Spinoza, just as it is virtue. One is powerful when one acts from one's own nature, and that only comes when one knows what one is doing and why one is doing it, namely when one's ideas are adequate. I have suggested that one's actions only "flow" when clarity is at the center of them. Virtually all the characteristics attributed to flow and gratification seem to me to depend upon clarity or "knowledge" (or "reason" as I interpret the passage above), including the ability to increase knowledge. If that claim is wrong about positive psychology, it is certainly not wrong about Spinoza.

But we do, at this juncture, run into a bit of a problem. First, Spinoza looks rather Platonic in equating knowledge and virtue, and this raises the old debate between Plato and Aristotle about the connection between knowledge and virtue. Plato equates the two, but Aristotle argued that another element, habituation, is needed as well.[21]

It does seem that there is reason for saying that Spinoza is not very interested in character as this term may be understood in some readings of Aristotle or positive psychology—that is, he is not particularly interested in character as habituated dispositions. In this understanding of character, character would seem to be a passive thing for Spinoza, because habituation is not a mode of adequate ideation. Indeed, part of Aristotle's point against Plato was that habituation was not particularly ideational at all. And on Spinoza's side of things, the world seems divided between the passive and the active with, unfortunately, the active being little in sight, for "it is rarely the case that men live by the guidance of reason" (E4P35Cor.2Schol.). This fact about the world would seem to suggest that the middle sort of person—who may not be virtuous by living as reason dictates, nor ignorant and morally incontinent, but habituated to virtue—is not possible in Spinoza's system. One is either active or passive, and while one may be a mixture of the two to varying degrees, there seem to be no secondary degrees of actuality that might correspond to a virtuous disposition.[22]

For my part, I do not think we should rush to judgment too quickly about the difference between Spinoza and Aristotle on this matter. Aristotle's conception of *eudaimonia* is one of *activity*, and as I read him I do not think his conception of activity is too far from Spinoza's own. Aristotle is certainly no stranger to celebrating knowledge, wisdom, and clarity in action, not to mention self-determination and activity in accordance with our nature.[23] It is furthermore not clear to me that Aristotle would disagree that a certain sort of habituation would be a passive condition. In this connection, it might be worth considering whether Aristotle could consider a distinction of dispositions: those dispositions that would be mere "habits" and those dispositions that might be on the order of "second natures." The former dispositions would be more passive because they represent more inertial forms of behavior. The latter form would be more active because the disposition was fully incorporated and integrated into the agent and thus had the marks required by Spinoza for considering an action "active." That is, these active dispositions are forms of unimpeded endeavoring stemming from the agent's own nature and understanding.

But even if habituation must be thought of only in passive terms, Spinoza—and Aristotle alike—might very well hold that if "living by the guidance of reason" is rare, we rely upon certain sorts of such positive passive states of character to a great degree in order to achieve any level of activity (E4P37Schol.2). These states might be thought of as anchors in the world which give us the stability to be more active in other areas, since our finitude does not allow us to be active in all. Thus, although we might consider various combinations of activity and passivity, both thinkers are nonetheless clear that some form of self-determination is at the center of what it means to live a "good" life and to be active.

In Aristotle, however, there is the sense that some people are superior to others, which, at least in his case, has a tendency to hierarchy.[24] Cooperation, by contrast, rather than superiority is the hallmark of Spinoza's interpersonal ethics and the key to enhanced power. Nevertheless, there is a distinction between the active and the passive individual, so how are they to interact? Do active individuals have more "rights" than passive individuals and therefore can do as they please with respect to them? It is first of all important to remind ourselves that there are not active people and passive people as the foregoing paragraphs might suggest. Each of us is a mixture of both and also passive in many different ways (E3P51). There is then a built-in reason to be skeptical of claims to inherent and systematic superiority of some over others, though of course relative superiority of some, at some times, and on some levels, is undoubtedly the case. Given this diversity of powers and adequacy, the sensible strategy would be to find ways of effectively utilizing the relative superiorities to the benefit of all. We have suggested that this comes from social cooperation.

Limitations to what might be mutually agreeable would come from the general rules of reason that must circumscribe the universe of mutually interested interactions and which must set some limits to allowable forms of interactions. Because human beings can find pleasure in virtually anything (E3P15), there is a need to neutralize or eliminate those agreements that are especially undermining of the process of forming mutually agreeable associations. People cannot, obviously, be allowed to agree to absolutely anything that might please them. The rules that circumscribe behavior and mutual agreement bring us again to the political as discussed in the first chapter. With respect to the ethical dimension of Spinoza's thought, we can see that actual cases of full activity are rare as he conceives them. More importantly, we have learned that activity is not going to serve as much of a basis for the social modeling of *practical* obligations or *practical* normative imperatives as it does with, say, Kant. In situations where passivity predominates, surrogates for activity in the form of cooperation by mutual agreement or enjoyment alone is the desired form of interaction or endeavoring for Spinoza. But we have seen that the active life, the life of ethical perfection, though not necessarily in contrast to morality, is in some significant sense beyond it[25] and not by any means concluded through social cooperation alone. There is a dimension beyond the social that characterizes Spinoza's ethics and that is the subject of our next chapter.

The main point of this chapter, then, is to point out that Spinoza has a different sort of ethics from the usual type. He has what we have labeled an ethics of immanence as opposed to the more usual forms that might fall into the categories of an ethics of transcendence or an ethics of propriety. An ethics of immanence is an ethics whose normative standards are derived almost exclusively within oneself by reference to one's nature, propensities, and circumstances. An ethics of transcendence is one where the normative standards are not derived from, and have no particular reference to, oneself uniquely and which function as norms *for* both individual and social action (Kant and Mill). An ethics of propriety is one where the normative standards also are not derived from and have no particular reference to, oneself uniquely and which function as norms *of* both individual and social action (Hume and Smith). In the former case, the norms operate as rules (e.g., the greatest happiness principle, or the categorical imperative) to which individuals should conform their behavior. In the case of an ethics of propriety, the norms are standards to which the individual more or less adheres and which may allow for varying degrees of approbation and disapprobation. In an ethics of transcendence, the norms are typically "rules of reason." In the case of an ethics of propriety, the norms are typically a cognized version of generalized social practices and their attendant evaluative parameters.

An ethics of immanence, by contrast, derives its norms neither from rules of reason nor from social practices, but in some way from the capacities, propensities, and circumstances of the active individual herself. Of course, all ethical approaches only count actions that are taken "voluntarily" as being actions of ethical import. In this way, all ethical approaches give the individual a primary role in the production of ethical value. But as I have tried to indicate above, in an ethics of immanence, there is no distance between, or separation of, the individual and the norms she should or does follow. This is not another version of making norms "one's own," but rather is something akin to the norms being of one's own making. Put this way, the proposition sounds subjectivist. However, an immanent ethics is only subjectivist in the very technical sense that universality is unimportant to it. Beyond that there is no necessary adherence to relativism, the absence of truth, or the absence of principles so often associated with subjectivism. Indeed, the demands of an ethics of immanence are generally more stringent than those associated with transcendence or propriety, for typically an ethics of immanence incorporates some mastery of these other two ethical forms before resolving itself into a norm of conduct for the individual in question.[26] We need to explore further this understanding of immanence, and thus we turn once more to the idea of activity itself.

Chapter Four

Freedom

It could be said that "freedom" for Spinoza is arguably the central concept and ultimate subject of his work. It is certainly the main message of his *Ethics* and the promise of that work. To this point we have gained some sense of what freedom might mean for Spinoza through the concept of activity. The following passage should remind us of the view of freedom with which we have been working:

> [W]e shall readily see the difference between the man who is guided only by emotion or belief and the man who is guided by reason. The former, whether he will or not, performs actions of which he is completely ignorant. The latter does no one's will but his own, and does only what he knows to be of greatest importance in life, which he therefore desires above all. So I call the former a slave and the latter a free man ... (E4P66Schol.)

On the surface, Spinoza's view seems simple enough: one is free when one lives the life of reason and not free to the degree one is ruled by emotion. Despite the apparent simplicity of the doctrine, there seem to be two basic ways to go about understanding Spinoza on this topic, both of which are aptly summarized in the following passage from a contemporary commentator on Spinoza:

> While Spinoza's system was integrated into the history of philosophy as one of
> the great systems, its author was misinterpreted as a thinker who stood in the

long tradition of those who sought ways to subordinate affects to reason, and who understood human freedom as the freedom from affects, i.e., as the reign of reason over affects. Contrary to this, the achievement of Spinoza was ... to show that human action is always and necessarily determined by affects. Even the free man's acts are caused by affects—albeit affects that are actions rather than passions.[1]

The (mis)understanding of Spinoza as someone who sought to subordinate the affects (often translated as "emotion") to reason is the first interpretation of "freedom" in his work as we saw in the preceding chapter. There are good reasons for this misinterpretation of Spinoza. He often talks as if this first way of understanding the relationship between the emotions (affects) and reason was the correct one. Indeed the passage from Spinoza just cited above seems to suggest this view. We, however, shall be adopting the second alternative—that "human action is always and necessarily determined by affects" even when one is "free." It is certainly the one that fits most closely with what we have been saying about Spinoza in the previous chapters. In those chapters we sought to continually clarify the meaning of activity and passivity in human conduct. With such a background it is easy enough to state simply that freedom is activity for Spinoza. It is, indeed, nothing more or less than this.

Only one being is fully active for Spinoza, and that is God. But a surprising amount of freedom is possible for humankind, if only we understand it in the second way of understanding freedom posed above. We need to accept as central to the human condition Spinoza's statement that "the essence of man is desire" (Def. of Emotions 1)[2] and then learn to recognize the most efficacious forms of desire. When we are finished we will realize that freedom truly is activity, pure and simple. It is not the control of some passions (passive ones) by others (active ones); it is not the struggle to transform the passive into the active; it is not the blocking of the passive by the active. It is simply activity itself. It is, in this respect, singularly unselfconscious, unlike the traditional doctrines that pit reason against passion and which therefore see reason as self-consciously exerting itself over the passive. It is as if passivity is simply replaced by activity itself. That is what we shall look into in this chapter. The idea being rejected is one that holds that freedom is control, so that human freedom would be the control over one's environment, whether that environment be oneself or one's surroundings. Freedom is not control of one's environment. It is being one's environment. Freedom is not control at all, for control suggests resistance. Freedom is irresistible activity.

Perhaps now we are ready to consider a further extension of our auto mechanic's example to help illustrate further the meaning of freedom. Imagine a situation where a person is driving along, let's say in a hurry to arrive somewhere, and the person's car suddenly and unexpectedly stalls out and will not restart by simply turning the key. We can easily imagine how a person who knows nothing about cars would act in this situation. Apart from the frustration that comes from the inevitable delay, one might expect a certain amount of anger, of swearing, of looking under the hood to no effect, of perhaps kicking the car, throwing up one's hands and the like. The point is, having no ideas, the person is completely at the mercy of his or her circumstances and emotions. The person would be, to say the least, completely passive. The "pain" and frustration experienced would perhaps only add to the person's ineptitude and ineffectiveness, for one's thinking is likely to become even more clouded and less focused in such a situation.

Notice in this connection another possibility: in the person's frustration and anger the person begins to poke randomly and pull at some of the wires under the hood of the car. Suppose in doing so there's some indication that the car might start again (e.g., the person gets back in and turns the key and some sort of sound is made). Now the pleasure that comes from this consequence will move the person to a "higher state of perfection"—that is, the person will continue to adjust those wires to start the car. But the person is still completely passive. Since the person has no real understanding of how the machine works, the noise that was heard may or may not be connected to the movement of wires. From this we can see that a person's endeavoring may be increased in a certain direction, but that person is still not "active" in Spinoza's sense and thus is not "free" either.

Contrast the foregoing scenario with one in which the person driving is quite knowledgeable about cars—say, our auto mechanic from the previous chapter. The frustration at the delay is likely to be the same, but there the similarity to the other case ends. This person may know by the sound of the way the car stalled out where the problem is likely to be. When he or she opens the hood it is with an understanding of what one is looking at and how the various parts function and are connected together. Attitudinally, the person will not be bandied about by various emotions, but will instead have emotions that would be closer to the category of confidence. The person will understand that there's a reason for the problem, what the likely alternatives are, and will approach the situation with a belief that he or she will be able to at least understand what to do, if not solve it right then and there. The feelings of confidence, efficacy, and focus all stem from the person's possession of adequate ideas. The person is not dwelling in confused, negative, and unhelpful emotions such as anger. Indeed, those unhelpful emotions soon get displaced, if present at all, by the more active emotions connected to knowing what one is doing and doing it.

Of course, most of us are neither so knowledgeable as the mechanic nor so ignorant as the completely hapless motorist. We may have some knowledge of cars, but not an extensive amount. But this is instructive too. Suppose we are passive and sitting there wallowing in the pains of our misfortune. Imagine what happens to us when we think of an idea, or a plan, for solving our problem. Our ineffective negative emotions start to get displaced and we begin to act on the idea. Having an idea or a plan is not the same as having an *adequate* idea or plan. But if the ideas that make up the plan are good ones, the endeavoring created will reinforce itself through success, and we will persist until the problem is solved. Emotionally we are focused on what furthers efficacy and with the further extension of ourselves into and over our environment. The less passive we are, the more our emotions are not of the type that impede our progress but give us increased motivation. This is why terms such as "perfection," "reality," "virtue," and "activity" are virtually synonymous for Spinoza. They all refer in some way to the power of something to exert itself efficaciously into its environment. And if we are allowed to speak of death as a terminal extreme of what is inefficacious, weak, and passive, we can see why Spinoza would say that "the free man thinks of death least of all things, and his wisdom is a meditation of life, not of death" (E4P67).

Two possible scenarios remain to be considered that relate to our example and our attempt to understand freedom and activity. In the first case, we can imagine a situation where the ignorant driver is randomly playing with the wires under the hood and manages (somehow) to get the car started and moves on. In the second case, we can imagine that the knowledgeable driver who is thoroughly familiar with the mechanical functioning of the car concludes that the car cannot be fixed with the tools at hand and that she is therefore stuck and unable to leave. Which of these two individuals is "freer" from a Spinozistic point of view? I think we already know what we are supposed to say in answer to this question—namely that the knowledgeable driver is freer because she possesses adequate ideas. But this seems counter-intuitive both to our common sense and to the way we have been discussing Spinoza. It seems contrary to Spinoza's doctrine, because the ignorant driver is nonetheless endeavoring further, while the knowledgeable driver is effectively stymied completely. It seems contrary to common sense for the same reason. The ignorant driver is at least getting his desires fulfilled.

It is important to understand, however, that freedom (or activity) for Spinoza is a term that applies to the *real* world, not the hypothetical one. The ignorant driver is no longer free because he is getting to where he wants to go. He is rather at a "higher state of perfection," to use Spinoza's expression about pleasure. That is to say, the person is being more successful in his pursuits, but not as a result of his own understanding. Such situations are simply not that much different from being lucky. So although at first, it seems somewhat counter-intuitive to think of driver going nowhere as freer than the one arriving at his destination, reflection suggests that we have misconstrued the comparison. The relevant comparison is between the ignorant driver getting somewhere and the ignorant driver being unable to move, and between the knowledgeable driver being stuck and the knowledgeable driver being able to travel. In both cases we can say that the person moving is freer, because in both cases the drivers are endeavoring successfully relative to themselves immobilized. They are both at a "higher state of perfection" when they are able to move towards their destinations.

But to make this comparison is to create hypothetical cases (where the cars are running). Using only real cases, it turns out to be unenlightening to compare the two individuals, except to make the point we are now making. Making the comparison is unhelpful because in reality all we can say is that one got moving and the other did not, and there is a set of causal explanations for that outcome. These causal patterns extend well beyond what the agent has any control over or even knows. So if we are interested in freedom, we must fall back on the definition of activity with which we have been working. With that definition we can only conclude that ignorant driver is not free, and the knowledgeable driver is. And once the example is stated clearly, it is no longer so counter-intuitive. For what we would say about these cases from the point of view of "common sense" is that although the ignorant driver was fortunate, he still is not free. He is taking advantage of what is happening to him, but not doing much himself.

The more significant lesson from all this is that, unlike Hobbes, freedom is not simply unimpeded motion for Spinoza.[3] It is not that unimpeded motion is unrelated to freedom. As we have seen, since we are moved by our emotions, then, *ceteris paribus,* being able to follow them would be a positive step towards freedom. But that positive step alone ignores the distinction between activity and passivity, for we have also seen that one can be unimpeded in either state. Apart, therefore, from the utility provided to us with respect to the active/passive distinction that comes by not thinking of freedom as simply unimpeded motion, we also gain the ability to say more about what it means to live the right kind of life than what is provided by "unimpeded motion." Provided we work within Spinoza's own definitions and categories, a discussion of the good life for Spinoza will not be as empty as "getting what one wants," as might be said about Hobbes. As we have noted already in a number of ways, there is immanence in Spinoza's philosophy that is more or less absent from doctrines such as Hobbes's. That immanence allows us to say more about what might constitute a free life. Yet, before we can draw any conclusions about the free—and we shall add "meaningful"—life, we need to mention one other important element in Spinoza's conception of things that we have deliberately skirted until now, but which is nonetheless necessary to our discussion—namely, the "third level of knowledge."

Knowledge and Action

We have left unmentioned to this point Spinoza's levels of knowledge so as not to find ourselves caught up in yet another facet of his philosophy that may take us too far from our main task of exploring Spinoza's humanistic conception of freedom. But we are at a stage now where mentioning the third level of knowledge can be helpful to us in understanding that freedom which is connected to what might also be thought of as Spinoza's the third level of the good. In general, Spinoza has three levels of knowledge (E2P40Schol.2). The first is a correct, but sensory grasp of some truth, received by the mind in a "fragmentary and confused manner." This level is what Spinoza calls "imagination." The second level is a form of reason which deals with common properties and general ideas of things. Finally, there is the third level about which there is considerable controversy,[4] but which grows out of the second level (E5P28). We are told that the "highest conatus of the mind and its highest virtue is to understand things by the third kind of knowledge." When we do this we "proceed from the adequate idea of certain of God's attributes to the adequate knowledge of the essence of things" (E5P25 & Proof). In this connection Margaret Wilson notes,

> Spinoza gives us some reason to suppose that what he has in mind is [at least in part] our coming to grasp intuitively the "force to persevere in existence" that defines the essence of singular things as a manifestation and consequence of God's power. Unfortunately—and exasperatingly—he says little else to elucidate this fundamental notion.[5]

Wilson's emphasis is one that is most useful to our project here. And without pretending, as she does not, that we are fully clear about the notion of the third kind of knowledge, Wilson's insight is worth a moment of our reflection.

We do not live in the world of static Platonic forms or Kantian noumenal objects which, like furniture in a room, are stationary and aloof. The objects in our environment have powers and forces of their own which assert themselves upon us in ways that are quite independent of their epistemic role in our minds. Whether we grasp them or not, they are there pushing at us, aiding our progress or wearing us down, providing obstacles or clearing our path. The problem then is one of learning how to make their powers our own, thus making us the agent pushing against *them*, so to speak. We learn, in other words, how to turn their power into an extension of our own person, thus using those powers to actually expand our own. By doing so we preserve and extend ourselves more effectively into the environment of objects in which we find ourselves. The problem with the second level of knowledge is that it is too universal. Spinoza's nominalism is one which forces us to realize, however, that at least at the modal level (i.e., the level of individuals), what is impinging upon us in the world is not a general type or general principle, but particular things and particular actions with particular natures.

Objects and actions cannot then be seen merely as instances of some general type, but must be seen as individuals, not exactly like others, however grouped they may be by the same general term. As such, these individuals have their own conatus, which if they are part of what populates the actual environment in which we act, must be understood in their *individual* capacity if their power is to work effectively with ours. So-called "theoretical knowledge" is never sufficient for effective action, because it pays no attention to the conatus exhibited by each individual. Learning from experience alone is somewhat more effective in this respect, but it suffers from two main defects: 1) it is limited to the cases experienced and thus does not readily benefit from any commonalities that are helpful when confronting new cases, and 2) it is too conservative, and thus ultimately limiting, for our incentive to learn more and expand our reach is not contained in the cases experienced. Indeed, our tendency would be to rest with what we know. The third level of knowledge, then, unites the general and the particular while at the same time urging us forward in our expansion of knowledge. "The more capable the mind is of understanding things by the third kind of knowledge, the more it desires to understand things by this same kind of knowledge" (E5P26).

Book V of the *Ethics* takes off from this proposition and presents to us a life that seems essentially contemplative and philosophical. Now whether the life of the mind is to be interpreted in this traditional contemplative way, thus embracing the Aristotelian paradox that what seems least active is actually most active, is open to debate.[6] As suggested earlier, we hold that Spinoza is not so quietistic and contemplative as he may appear under many readings.[7] Be that as it may, our domain of reference for the moment is ordinary practical action, since we are speaking of moral, political, and personal actions taken in the world by individuals acting among others. Given this focus—and again in the spirit of Aristotle—we may have to think of Spinozistic activity in this context as a "second best" life, if philosophical contemplation is finally the quintessential form of activity for Spinoza. Even so, the practical life is clearly a life from which Spinoza did not mean to *exclude* the third level of knowledge (E4P35Cor.2&Schol.). In addition, it is important to notice that although the purging of our passive emotions is a Stoic sort of project, and Spinoza was certainly influenced by the Stoics, in the end Spinoza seeks not to purge our emotions and withdraw us from the world, but exactly the opposite—to induce in us emotions that are effective for action in the world.[8] As noted at the opening of this chapter, Spinoza does not want to purge emotions but to urge us to more active ones. Moreover, passive emotions, as we have seen, are not necessarily contrary to our perfection.

With respect to what is not associated with the body as emotions often are, namely ideas, they carry with them their own forms of perfection, which means their own power of affirmation and negation (E2P49Schol.). We noted before that a powerful and clear idea is presumably one that leads us on to others. A confused and weak one is one that leaves us unable to give a precise account of the idea or leaves us without an ability to integrate it well with other ideas. If then our essence is appetite or desire, which unites the conatus of our ideas with that of our body (pleasure and pain), then ideas about action will only tend to withdraw us from the world if they are in some way defective, inadequate, and painful. Effective, adequate, and pleasurable ideas would encourage *more* involvement in the world around us. The free person thinks of death least of all things. The life of the mind, assuming in this case the mind's object is action, would not issue in quietistic withdrawal but in ever more enthusiastic action.

But even granting that quietism does not constitute Spinoza's message of freedom or salvation, is it nonetheless the case that Spinoza is advocating the philosophical life as the only truly "active" one? In other words, the question here is related to one raised above: is Spinoza doing the same thing as Aristotle (or some interpretations of Aristotle) in holding a) the philosophic life qualifies as "active" and engaged, and b) thereby suggesting that it is also the only fully active life because the only one devoted exclusively to exercising reason? The temptation certainly exists to answer these questions with a "yes," if for no other reason than Spinoza's own conduct in his own life was the quintessential life of a philosopher. Few adults have been so disengaged from the practical and as contemplative of philosophical matters as Spinoza in his own life.[9]

The idea that both Spinoza's doctrine and his own example lead us inevitably to the conclusion that the degree to which one is a philosopher is the degree to which one is active and blessed seems to be the norm in reading Spinoza. Recently, for example, in her wonderfully engaging book about Spinoza, Rebecca Goldstein puts this interpretation well when she argues that,

> From out there, the remotest point from which to behold the world, the fact of who one is within the world seems to disappear; one can gain no purchase on it. This is what happens when one assumes the view *sub specie aeternitatis*, and this is the view that Spinoza recommends to us as the means of attaining salvation.[10]

Goldstein describes the perspective needed for salvation as the "view from nowhere." Later on, she further emphasizes the point with the following:

> Salvation is achieved by bringing the vision of the *causa sui*—the vast and infinite system of logical entailments of which each of us is but one entailment—into one's very own conception of oneself, and, with that vision reconstituting oneself, henceforth living, as it were, outside of oneself. The point, for Spinoza, is not to become insiders, but rather outsiders. The point is to become ultimate outsiders.[11]

Both these passages taken together suggest the philosophical or contemplative life as the most "active" one or the one most in accord with the requirements for salvation, perhaps because it approaches the divine most closely. The philosophical life is, of all lives, the one most concerned with universals and the only one that cares to take the perspective of *sub specie aeternitatis*. In Goldstein's account there is almost a sense of a disappearing self as we become more and more outside our own particularity. The point of view of eternity is the point of view recommended by Spinoza for salvation: "it is clear … that our mind, insofar as it understands, is an eternal mode of thinking" (E5P40Schol.); and "from this we clearly understand in what our salvation or blessedness or freedom consists, namely, in the constant and eternal love toward God" (E5P36Schol.). The perspective of eternity coupled with the example of Spinoza's own life, the fact that he is read by other philosophers, and the continual exercise of reason by the exercise of philosophy all conspire together to suggest some form of contemplative existence as being the way of salvation.

The reader of Spinoza is led to conclude that the traditional philosophical life is best because of passages like the following:

> Therefore it is of the first importance in life to perfect the intellect, or reason, as far as we can, and the highest happiness or blessedness for mankind consists in this alone. For blessedness is nothing other than that self-contentment that arises from the intuitive knowledge of God. Now to perfect the intellect is also nothing other than to understand God and the attributes and actions of God that follow from the necessity of his nature. Therefore for the man who is guided by reason, the final goal, … is that by which he is brought to an adequate conception of himself and of all things that can fall within the scope of his understanding. (E4App.#4)

It would, of course, seem that only the philosopher could so perfect his or her intellect in the way just described. Practical people, certainly, would be unable to find the time for such perfection. If not the discipline of philosophy itself, an intellectual life would at least seem to be necessary for blessedness. But putting aside, for the moment, the example of Spinoza's own life, such inferences may all be too quick. There is no *necessary* connection between the intellectual life and blessedness as Spinoza here describes it. There are first of all plenty of intellectuals who fail to have "adequate conception[s] of [themselves] and of all things that can fall within the scope of [their] understanding." Even if we only allow those who do have such adequate conceptions to fall within the category of "intellectual" or "philosopher," there is no recommendation in this passage, or virtually any other in the *Ethics*, that explicitly identifies the philosophical or intellectual life as the ideal one.

Indeed, although we are tempted to read the "can" in the last line of the passage just cited as a call to philosophy—for doesn't "what can fall within the scope" mean everything, and aren't philosophers the only ones who cognize everything?—we do not have to take it as such. We could read the "can" in Spinozistic fashion to mean all those things connected to the trajectory I am now taking and which cannot be otherwise. In other words, we are not talking of an abstracted "can" disconnected from all contexts and understood universally, but rather a "can" connected with what I am actually doing and pursuing now. With the abstracted "can," of course, one would in principle know no boundaries to what might have some connection to what one is doing. But that point applies to everything, and once one takes seriously Spinoza's other principle that we are finite modes, then what "can" fall within our scope is largely defined by our personal trajectory and that could be almost anything.

So must we draw the conclusion that the contemplative philosophical life is the paradigm of activity according to Spinoza? It shall be my contention that something akin to the opposite way of living is the implication, if not the exact prescription, of Spinoza's arguments. Instead of becoming "outsiders," the final freedom is to become truly "insiders." For the freest being there would be no outside, and ironically—given that Goldstein is right that we must go "outside" to gain salvation—we must be outside only so that we can finally be inside. The "view from nowhere" is precisely where we do not want to be, though we must in some way go there to finally arrive "inside." Philosophers certainly have certain advantages over other pursuits—the ability to move themselves "outside" being chief among them; but virtually any other occupation has the advantage of helping one to be more of an "insider" by having its own objective focus. In this regard, philosophy as it is usually understood and practiced, can actually be a hindrance to insidedness, since it always pulls towards the universal and not the particular. But here we are being too obscure and abstract. Let's probe this a bit further by talking about what might be said against the contemplative life as a model of the best form of life.

The Best Life as the Meaningful Life

At the end of *Authentic Happiness*, Martin Seligman struggles with the question of what it means to live a "meaningful life."[12] His concluding sentence is interesting for our purposes: "the meaningful life adds one more component [to the good life of gratification]: using these same [signature] strengths to forward knowledge, power, or goodness. A life that does this is pregnant with meaning, and if God comes at the end, such a life is sacred."[13] Spinoza might be willing to say something similar, except that God would not be coming at the end but imbuing each act along the way. Nonetheless, forwarding knowledge, power, and goodness are vintage Spinozistic aims and would be exhibited in any meaningful or free life. But is any pursuit as good as any other provided knowledge, power, and goodness are furthered in some active way? Is the contemplative life actually most forwarding of knowledge, power, and goodness? Antonio Damasio also offers us some reflections on this same issue. The general context of meaningfulness is described by Damasio as follows:

> Many people appear to require something more out of life beyond moral and law-abiding conduct; beyond the satisfaction of love, family, friendships, and good health; beyond the rewards that come from doing well whatever job one chooses ... beyond the pursuit of one's pleasures and the accumulation of possessions; and beyond an identification with country and humanity. ... Whether we articulate this need clearly or confusedly, it amounts to a yearning to know where we come from and where we are going, mostly the latter perhaps.[14]

When thinking specifically about Spinoza on the question of meaningfulness, Damasio notes the following two roads to salvation that Spinoza offers:

> The accessible road requires a virtuous life in a virtuous *civitas*, obedient to the rules of a democratic state and mindful of God's nature, somewhat indirectly, with the help of some of the Bible's wisdom. The second road requires all that is needed by the first and, in addition, intuitive access to understanding that Spinoza prized above all other intellectual instruments, and which is itself based on abundant knowledge and sustained reflection.[15]

Spinoza's first road to salvation is obviously the road described in the preceding passage that is prior to the longing for "something more."

In previous chapters we might have described such a life at this first level as a form of passivity, but one in accord with reason. For our purposes here the more problematic move, then, is the intellectualist interpretation Damasio gives to finding that "something more" in Spinoza. For Damasio, the road of intellectual contemplation, while accurately describing Spinoza's view of the matter, is too isolated from human society and not sufficiently in tune with the real suffering (our own and that of others) that exists around us. No doubt Seligman would agree. There seems to be something too quietistic and otherworldly about the contemplative life to have it serve as a model for the unqualifiedly best life. Must we see Spinoza's doctrine as implying detachment from the world however active we may regard intellection as being?

I believe the answer to this last question is, no. Spinoza defines salvation in terms of freedom from the passive emotions. But the solution he offers is one, if interpreted in the common intellectualist fashion, which is not strictly speaking the obverse of passivity. Strictly speaking, we would be free, not when we live the contemplative life, but rather when we are active. In Spinoza's three levels of knowledge (sense, reason, and "intuition"), the intellectual love of God—which gives us the apparently intellectualist reading of Spinoza's "second road" to salvation—is the third and highest level of knowledge. Yet the second level can also contain adequate ideas (E2P40Schol.2) and thus be active as well. But since this is all that is really needed for freedom or what Spinoza calls "blessedness" (and what we are including here under the rubric of "meaningful"), it is at least theoretically possible that there are a number of possible "free" lives besides the contemplative one. All that is required for freedom is activity, and while contemplation may qualify as active, that is some distance from saying it is the *only* form of activity. With this in mind, it might, for example, be possible to consider as an active, meaningful, and free life the one described by positive psychology to the effect that exercising the signature strengths through the core virtues oriented towards something larger than oneself is simply all that is needed for a meaningful life. In this case we would then say that activity is inherently outwardly directed because it must be linked to something larger than oneself. Why not rest contented with this inference?

There does seem to me to be something missing still, and that is simply that it is not clear what outwardness or becoming part of something larger is invoking to add meaningfulness to life. What is missing so far is something that is not unconnected to the very intellectualist orientation we have been so desirous of setting aside. What I think is tacit in positive psychology's formulation of meaningfulness, somewhat explicit in Damasio's "additional element" beyond the good life, and very explicit in Spinoza's third kind of knowledge is the need for intellectual integration.[16] Intellectual integration is what we must add to the activities in which we engage, however enmeshed in outwardness or larger contexts they may be. We seek to *understand* how what we do fits into a larger whole—not just to *be* a part of something larger than ourselves. The active mind is always struggling to see connections, and the active life to find a role within them. Religion is certainly one way to provide an integrated story for us to consider. There may be a number of other ways as well. Indeed, I am pushing us towards the conclusion that we can find freedom, meaningfulness, and blessedness in a virtually limitless variety of human activities. In this respect, Spinoza is launching a frontal assault on the Aristotelian distinction between the intellectual and the practical life. For Spinoza there are only active and passive lives and the form of intellection is the same in them all.

In the case of positive psychology, Seligman ends *Authentic Happiness* with the idea that meaningfulness may be recognizing our contribution to the positive direction of the course of human evolution that comes from adopting positive frameworks in life. Damasio suggests that integration would require us to combine intellectualist elements with more worldly activities, facing squarely the prospect of mortality.[17] I do not pretend to have better answers than these to offer at this stage, but it seems to me that the quest for integration is a feature of the active mind and thus must be common to all such "solutions." At some level, we try to find ways to understand ourselves within and through the larger wholes that affect our experience. Doing so is an intellectual act and one that carries with it more plausibility and legitimacy in proportion to the adequacy of the ideas that make it up. Our lives can thus have meaning even if our integrative acts do not quite put all the pieces of the whole together in a complete final picture. Our lives will not be free and meaningful if we are confused, passive, disengaged, or distracted, or if we simply ignore completely the question of "how it all fits." This, rather than simply the contemplative life, is the interpretation I would like, in the end, to give to Spinoza himself. It is not necessarily the quiescent life of the philosopher we must imitate, but the philosopher's call to understanding and integration.

> Therefore for the man who is guided by reason, the final goal, that is, the highest Desire whereby he strives to control all the others, is that by which he is brought to an adequate conception of himself and of all things that can fall within the scope of his understanding. (E4App.#4)

The integration needed for freedom will take the form of an intuitive grasp of a complex network of interconnections within which one navigates one's life and of which one is a part. Since God is everything for Spinoza, that intuition is certainly an *amor intellectualis Dei*. But it is conceivable that the intellectual love of God is not a separate intellectual act, apprehension, or state of being, but rather any integrative active intuition itself. Thus to understand, and from that understanding to act efficaciously within one's environment, is a form of blessedness, salvation, or love of God. In this way of interpreting reason and intellection, there is little that suggests either transcendence or a particular mode of living.

It is in the fifth part of the *Ethics* that Spinoza tells us he is going to teach us what leads to freedom.

> I pass finally to that part of the *Ethics* which concerns the method or way leading to freedom. In this part, then, I shall be dealing with the power of reason, pointing out the degree of control reason has over the emotions, and then what is freedom of mind, or blessedness, from which we shall see how much to be preferred is the life of the wise man to the life of the ignorant man. Now we are not concerned here with the manner or way in which the intellect should be perfected, nor yet with the science of tending the body so that it may correctly perform its functions. The latter is the province of medicine, the former logic. Here then, as I have said, I shall be dealing only with the power of the mind or reason. (E5Pref.)

Unfortunately, other than some of the opening propositions, which seem to largely reiterate points made in some of the earlier parts of the *Ethics*, the fifth part has been a source of controversy among scholars and relatively obscure in its meaning. Beyond noting once again that developing reason and controlling the emotions is our aim, what is perhaps striking about at least some of the opening propositions of Part V is the importance put on integration. We are told in Proposition 8, for example, that "the greater the number of causes that simultaneously concur in arousing an emotion, the greater the emotion" (E5P8). Following that we are told that "an emotion that is related to several different causes ... is less harmful ... than if we were affected by another equally great emotion which is related to only one or to a few causes" (E5P9). In addition, "in proportion as a mental image is related to more things, the more frequently does it occur ... and the more it engages the mind" (E5P11). Given that "images are more readily associated with those images that are related to things which we clearly and distinctly understand than they are to others" (E5P12), the more adequate our ideas the more associations we can draw. These last propositions are followed by one that says, "the mind can bring it about that all the affections of the body—that is, images of things—be related to the idea of God" (E5P14). God then is the context in which all the images, emotions, and ideas we have can be related to each other provided our ideas are clear and distinct enough (adequate) to see the various connections.

That act of seeing the connections just is the intellectual love of God for Spinoza. But more importantly with respect to what we are discussing here, that act of drawing connections through ideas, which is only possible if they are adequate, is the act of transforming passivity into activity. Despite Spinoza's language at times, the process here is not particularly one of countering one emotion with another (though that tool can be used too), but rather of transforming passive emotions into active ones by increasing the adequacy of our integrated ideas. The more adequate our ideas, the more we are impelled by them and the more they are our own. Knowledge coupled with compelling desire is efficacious action or freedom. But knowledge is about the interconnection of things and ideas adequately understood. Of course, we cannot *see* those interconnections unless our ideas are adequate, and, if our ideas are adequate, we cannot be confused by such things as passive emotions; hence the result is freedom.

In a way, then, the degree to which we can integrate is a measure of the degree to which we can be considered free. We do not, however, have to do this integration perfectly in order to reap its benefits.

> Hence it follows that that mind is most passive whose greatest part is constituted by inadequate ideas, so that it is characterized more by passivity than by activity. On the other hand, that mind is most active whose greatest part is constituted by adequate ideas, so that even if the latter mind contains as many inadequate ideas as the former, it is characterized by those ideas which are attributed to human virtue rather than by those that point to human weakness. (E5P20Schol.)

It is not then the presence of the passive ideas one possesses that makes one unfree, but rather the extent to which those ideas are influencing one's conduct. I may, for example, have numerous confused ideas about organic chemistry, but since I not only do not do organic chemistry, nor have virtually any engagement with doing chemistry of any kind, the possession of these ideas is relatively harmless. It would, however, be completely mistaken on my part to suppose that the ideas I do have that are adequate have no connection to ideas that are connected to organic chemistry. Moreover, having inadequate ideas about organic chemistry will certainly cause problems for me if I do move into areas where knowledge of organic chemistry will make my actions more efficacious. Indeed, one of the indications of one's love of God in Spinoza's sense is precisely the *continual* striving to transform passive ideas into adequate ones, which, at the same time, would bring one from emotional passivity to activity.

A number of propositions in Part V of the *Ethics* (e.g., propositions 25–36) are devoted to showing that the highest form of intellection is through knowledge of the third kind. With this sort of knowledge we are freest and our ideas most adequate. These propositions are preceded—I would say introduced—by a seemingly innocuous proposition that is easily skipped over as one progresses to apparently meatier ones that follow. This proposition says simply: "the more we understand particular things, the more we understand God" (E5P24). The proof for this proposition is even simpler. It tells us that this is evident from E1P25Cor. When we turn to that proposition we find Spinoza saying, "particular things are nothing but affections of the attributes of God, that is, modes wherein the attributes of God find expression in a definite and determinate way" (E1P25Cor.). Although the E1P25Cor. is supportive of E5P24, the "proof" does not seem compelling at first. For proposition 24 says "the more" we understand particulars, but presumably particulars are not all there are—there are at least attributes and a substance as well. Why isn't knowing more about those things a way to greater understanding of God? One would especially think so if the philosophical life were the best one!

Spinoza's proof is only a proof if we take it very seriously, that is, if we hold that the universe of things with which we interact is indeed only one of particulars. It is fashionable today in Spinoza scholarship to reject individualism in Spinoza whether it be in politics or metaphysics.[18] This tendency, however, is one that is being at least partially challenged here. Our endeavors are among particulars and more importantly our ideas issue in actions which are themselves particulars. Indeed, part of the point of this chapter is to suggest that unless our ideas do issue in particular actions of some sort, they are not yet adequate. Adequacy does not come from holding a true idea, but from exercising it. That is why Spinoza is less than enthusiastic about the second level of knowledge being adequate—that level has a tendency to remain in the form of universals. By contrast, the third level does not even exist unless we can apply the knowledge of the essence of God's attributes to the essence of particular things.[19]

Because Spinoza is more a nominalist than a traditional realist, there are no universal essences, making the "essence of particular things" a matter of individuals. This is not empiricism. We do not "understand" the essence of things by perceiving them. But by acting among them and relating them to each other, we will come to understand their natures and how those natures are connected to and affect ourselves and other things within the path of our endeavors. There can be, pace Aristotle and most of the philosophical tradition, no "best life" in the sense of there being one activity that supersedes all others in terms of its goodness, its proximity to God, its closeness to the eternal, or its elevation above other tasks. The blessed life is not so much a matter of what one does as to *how* one does what one does. Here what is required is that one exhibits all the marks of activity as we have discussed them here and in the previous chapters. The only constraints on what is to count as an activity that results in blessedness come from the social propositions of the *Ethics* (e.g., E4P35ff). That is to say, one can do virtually anything and achieve blessedness so long as one recognizes the value of his fellow human beings, integrates herself among them, and seeks cooperative and beneficial relationships with them (e.g., E4P36, 40). One could not, therefore, attain blessedness through crime. Beyond that, there are virtually no constraints. Plumbing could conceivably be as much a possible road to blessedness, salvation, and freedom as philosophy!

How then might we tie up the various strands of argument we have been advancing to a summary conclusion? First of all it seems correct to say that in order to live a meaningful life we must, for Spinoza, become a part of something larger than ourselves. Of course, just by existing that is true, given our limited nature and tiny spot in the vast universe of which we are part. But as we have discussed it here, being part of something larger means seeing ourselves actively networked to patterns of activity within our environment that extend well beyond us. We are not merely one atom among others when active, but an individual understood now as a being acting from its own nature. This means two things: 1) our insignificance with respect to the universe considered *sub specie aeternitatis* can be a unique form of meaningfulness when considered from our point of view when active,[20] and 2) we are only "networked" when active. In a passive condition we are essentially disconnected from our environment and become a mere effect of other active powers. The object is thus to bring our environment into ourselves through the integration of ideas and thus act from within to the outside. We become free because we become the center of our own network of connections, rather than being a node of some other network. We do this, as we shall discuss more fully in the next chapter, without any of the characteristics we would normally associate with being "self-centered." The experience of this active centrality is one of moving among the particulars that make up our environment with such clarity and focus that they seem, and perhaps are, a part of us rather than we of them. When we achieve this fluidity of endeavoring within the world around us, we are what we have described here and elsewhere as "active" and for that reason we become blessed. We are blessed because to be engaged in activity is in itself testimony to our taking the essence of God and applying it to the essence of things. This conception of ourselves within our world is a truly transformative and modern one. We aspire not to a final cause or a transcendent realm but to immanence. This conception of the move towards immanence is Spinoza's revolutionary introduction of modernity. To appreciate the various ways humankind has been lumbering towards Spinoza's vision is now the subject of our next chapter.

Chapter Five

Modernity, God, and Man

> Now let us imagine ... a tiny worm living in the blood, capable of distinguishing by sight the particles of blood—lymph, etc.—and of intelligently observing how each particle, on colliding with another, either rebounds or communicates some degree of its motion, and so forth. That worm would be living in the blood as we are living in our part of the universe. ...
>
> —*Spinoza* (Letter 32, to Henry Oldenburg)
>
> What does a fish know about the water in which it swims?
>
> —Einstein

As we noted in the introduction, Spinoza is credited with being modern on many fronts. Yet in this chapter we shall concentrate on two concepts which not only encompass components of many of the others we have explored, but also seem to be most central to Spinoza's modernity as it relates to his humanism. One of the concepts concerns Spinoza's continual drive to empower us. I have called this perspective simply "immanence."[1] Immanence not only incorporates elements of Spinoza's project from metaphysics to politics, but it is especially connected to the concepts of freedom and action with which we have been mainly working. In short, immanence has been the necessary and sufficient condition for self-determination, or the "action" part of us as individual acting agents. This is to say once again that our reading of Spinoza places successful agency at the center of Spinoza's entire project. Though we are not the center of the universe, we are the point of his philosophizing. In this respect, Spinoza's project is *essentially* ethical, not in the sense that it seeks to conform itself to, or to illuminate, some moral order, but in the sense that its purpose is the promotion of human well-being. Immanence is the path to well-being. Its origins, however, lie well beyond us, which brings us to our next main concept.

It might be said that entering the modern world meant leaving a human-centered universe. To this statement one could immediately object that the pre-modern universe was not human, but God-centered. Yet God (or the gods) was looking down upon or taking care of *us* in that pre-modern worldview. In addition, the physical cosmology was generally earth-centered with the heavenly bodies revolving around the earth.[2] Consequently, however expansive the universe or God's nature may have been, human beings were at its center being judged, nurtured, saved, damned, encouraged, or simply looked after by the God or gods that ruled it. Pre-modern *classical* antiquity may have lessened the autonomy and power of human beings in the face of their gods, and thus made them more vulnerable to the whims of those gods, but there was nonetheless a close relationship between the two. Similarly, the Judeo-Christian tradition may have accorded human beings more autonomy, but their God too was no less close to them. With the advent of modernity, however, the universe began to expand away from us. The cosmology first became helio-centric but eventually came to the position that the earth, its sun, and its solar system were not actually the center of anything. In addition, explanations of events in terms of God's intentions, desires, goals, or punishments became less and less convincing or unnecessary in the face of modern science. We increasingly moved from pre-modern womb-like security in a universe that cared about us, to being an infinitesimal part of a complex, impersonal, and blind confluence of forces. The question was no longer what God wants us to do, but simply how can we even keep anything like the traditional God in the picture at all?

But the issue did not rest simply upon theological or cosmological perspectives. The social world was changing also. Although colonialism, and thus the possibility of empire, continued much as it had in antiquity, modernity ushered in competing colonial powers as a result of international trade. There was not just Rome as in the past, but a Spain, an England, a Portugal and a France—and that ignores the Far and Middle East. New trade routes opened vast markets which softened the edge of any empire trying to control them. Economies began to modernize, which meant not only an increasing decentralization and complexity of international economies, but similar effects on domestic ones. It was difficult to maintain a central place in the world as a country, and even more so as a town, village, or city. As people's horizons expanded, their security of place and their particular importance to any global perspective diminished.

Consequently, as the universe increasingly distanced itself from our centrality as human beings generally, or as individuals in particular, we became increasingly anxious about our place within that universe. Some concluded we were alone and had no special place whatsoever; others tried to hold on to the idea that we were, in some significant respect, still central, even if the physical cosmology and economic modernization suggested otherwise. Either way, the problem was the same: what can we say about ourselves in the face of this decreasing significance? We felt it on the individual level as well as on the level of communities, nations, and humankind in general. From Spinoza's day to our own, the march of time has not diminished its trend in this direction. Indeed, the trend has increased, culminating perhaps with Darwin and the apparent devolution of ourselves as a species, given our origins in the lower primates rather than a transcendent being. Thus, the second main concept of modernity, ushered in by Spinoza who more clearly than anyone else saw its nature, is what I shall call "insignificance." In the pre-modern world, the centrality of human beings within the universe effectively gave them great significance. The entire trend of modernity has been in the opposite direction. The task before the modern human being, then, is to find a way to grasp the implications of insignificance.

The fact of insignificance was thoroughly recognized by Spinoza and for the first time laid before us. It was a message we did not want to hear. The intellectual classes especially were often no more receptive to this message than others, despite their critical role as instruments of the message itself. For part of what seems to happen in modern complex societies is the increasing irrelevance of intellectuals to the functioning of society, at least outside the sciences. In any case, Spinoza is certainly laying out the path that must be taken to meet the reality of insignificance, with his message to us being: face squarely the reality of insignificance if you wish to be free of its effects most troubling to humans. We can begin our understanding of that message by looking at some key components of Spinoza's metaphysics.

The Metaphysics of Immanence

We have said little to this point about Spinoza's metaphysics. Indeed, we have proceeded in virtually the reverse order Spinoza himself does in his main treatise, the *Ethics*. There he starts with the central concepts of God, substance, and nature, and moves towards human freedom later in the book. That approach is, of course, correct logically and substantively. Our being and prospects are a function of what is described by those central metaphysical concepts. But our approach here has been dictated by the fact that we have chosen to focus upon and emphasize Spinoza's humanism. Still, since our humanness is itself a function of these more fundamental concepts, they must be given at least some consideration. By the same token, we cannot hope to give an adequate account of Spinoza's rather complex metaphysics and its related theories in a single short chapter. Instead, our hope is to give enough of an introduction so that we see both the implications of insignificance and why immanence is the only model of action connected with it.

Set out in the "geometrical fashion" of definitions, axioms, propositions, and proofs, the first book of the *Ethics* concerns God. God, however, comes to be understood first in terms of another concept with which Spinoza begins, namely "substance." Substance itself has two other associated concepts, "attribute" and "mode." Along with God, it is perhaps best just to lay Spinoza's opening definitions before us:

> Def. 3: By substance I mean that which is in itself and is conceived through itself; that is, that the conception of which does not require the conception of another thing from which it has to be formed.

Def. 4: By attribute I mean that which the intellect perceives of substance as constituting its essence.

Def. 5: By mode I mean the affections of substance, that is, that which is in something else and is conceived through something else.

Def. 6: By God I mean an absolutely infinite being, that is, substance consisting of infinite attributes, each of which expresses eternal and infinite essence.

For the moment, let's ignore definitions 4 and 5 and concentrate on 3 and 6. We will come back to 4 and 5, however. Definition 6 seems to largely fit our ordinary understanding of what we mean by "God." Definition 3, by contrast, looks very obscure at first, especially to anyone not trained in philosophy. Yet after reading the definition a few times, one comes to see that whatever substance is, we're not going to understand it in terms of anything else. Instead, we are somehow going to understand everything else in terms of it. Substance is where everything comes from and to which everything is ultimately referred or dependent upon. There's nothing outside of it, and there's nothing else to explain what it is other than itself. Of course, once one begins thinking about substance in this way, substance starts looking a lot like what at least many people would ordinarily say about God!

That is precisely what Spinoza does in the opening propositions of the first book of the *Ethics*—he links substance and God together so that they are both names for the same thing. One notices also that the definition of God has a lot to do with infinity. Spinoza shows that substance is infinite (E1P8). We tend additionally to think that there can only be one of the kind of God Spinoza defines, so Spinoza proves that there cannot be more than one substance and that it couldn't have come from anything other than itself (E1P5–6). In addition, Spinoza formally links God and substance together (E1P11). Other concepts, such as existence and self-causation, have helped along the way, but the important idea for our purposes is that everything whatsoever, including God or substance itself, is encompassed by this concept expressed by the two terms "substance" and "God." But those terms do not quite give us the picture we need. For that picture, the terms "attribute" and "mode" are also required.

As we see in its definition, an attribute describes the essence of a substance. Whatever it means to describe a substance must be done through the attributes of the substance. Since God or substance is infinite, whatever the attributes of God or substance are, they must also be infinite. Moreover, it turns out that God or substance would not only have attributes that are infinite, but also infinitely many infinite attributes (E1P10–11). Thus, if we could give a description of one of these attributes—say "thought"—that description would mean, when applied to God or substance, that thought was infinite in God or substance. The idea that God's thoughts are applicable to everything that exists is probably not too far off from what most people would intuitively say about God. What Spinoza adds, however, is the idea that there are infinitely many *different* attributes of the same God or substance. It's like saying God or substance is infinite in both "length" and "breadth," although since we mentioned "thought," those terms used in this context are of course metaphors, not actual descriptions. Still, we can imagine on the one hand a *line* of thought, and we can imagine on the other a *range* of thoughts. God or substance would be infinite in both ways (not to mention infinitely many others).

Within "thought" we might be more comfortable talking about "thoughts." A "line of thought" is generally another name for a string of discrete thoughts. These discrete thoughts might more generally be called "modes" of thought. To be a mode of thought would be to be this or that thought. That's the idea behind the definition of "mode" Spinoza gives, noted above. The "affections of substance" used in Definition 5 are the *particular* manifestations of substance. Of course, those manifestations must be understood in a certain way. In this case we are considering them as kinds of thoughts. However, given what Spinoza has said about substance or God and attributes, there are an infinite numbers of ways in which God or substance may manifest itself (E1P16). Thus, there are also an infinite number of things that can be said about any given manifestation (E1P25Cor.). In this case, we're just talking about one such way—the manifestation as a thought of some sort. Although there are an infinite number of possible ways to consider any particular manifestation, our limited nature only allows us to really speak of the manifestations of two attributes, thought and extension (matter) (E2P1–2).[3] So when we talk about things in the world around us, we do so in terms of something being either a mode of thought, or of matter, or both.

Now that we have a rough idea of substance, attribute, and mode, we can look with particular interest to the 18th proposition of the first book of the *Ethics*: "God is the immanent, not the transitive, cause of all things." Though the meaning of this proposition is worked out in many successive propositions (as well as beyond book one), we can move to the point immediately. Remembering that there is nothing outside of God (or substance) and that everything that is must be understood in terms of God, this proposition is telling us that God is not simply something upon which everything depends and who makes it possible for things to do anything that they do or be anything that they are. Spinoza's point is actually more radical: everything actually *is* God (or substance). Indeed, how could it be otherwise? If God is truly infinite in infinite ways, and there's nothing outside of God or independent of God, then what makes the most sense is to see the things around us, including ourselves, as simply particular manifestations of God (or substance). To say otherwise would be to give something some independence from God. But that itself would mean that God faces some limit, namely, something that is not God, and that thing would throw up a boundary—or limit—to what God is. God's all-encompassing infiniteness would not be so all-encompassing or infinite in that case (E1P14). It is more plausible to think in terms of the one substance or God expressing itself in particular or modal ways than it is to suppose there is something that God or substance is not. But, of course, in saying all this, proposition 18 makes immanence an *essential* feature of all that is, not to mention an essential feature of Spinoza's philosophical system.

An idea often associated with Spinoza is the idea of "*deus sive natura*" or "God or nature" (E1App.; E4Pref.). The idea is quite simple: God and nature are interchangeable terms for Spinoza. Consequently, we actually have three terms that turn out to be identical in meaning and reference: substance, God, and nature. The significance of this equation of God and substance with nature is, at least, a reinforcement of immanence. Since God and nature are the same, there is no separation of God from nature. God didn't create the natural order; God *is* the natural order (and it is God). A whole host of interesting and controversial ideas seem to follow from this equation, some of which we shall mention in a moment. But one thing we immediately tend to associate with nature is the idea of causality. There are two points of importance here. First, as to nature as a whole, it didn't come from anywhere, but is self-caused (E1P7). If it sounds strange to think of nature as self-caused, we are free to substitute "God" for "nature," which to some ears might make the idea less foreign. Secondly, if God is everything and nothing is not God (E1P15), then God is the efficient cause of everything (E1P25,26). But if that is true, that would seem to mean that God is the cause of evil, that God is material, that anything we do is caused by God, which itself seems to mean we have no freedom of choice or independence of God. Indeed, these conclusions do follow for Spinoza. He tells us quite clearly, for example, "Nothing in nature is contingent, but all things are from the necessity of the divine nature determined to exist and to act in a definite way" (E1P29). And when it comes to human beings in particular, Spinoza says that each of us "follows the common order of Nature, and obeys it" (E4P4Cor.).

Finally, all the points we have been making above seem well summarized in these words from Spinoza:

> I have now explained the nature and properties of God: that he necessarily exists, that he is one alone, that he is and acts solely from the necessity of his own nature, that he is the free cause of all things and how so, that all things are in God and are so dependent on him that they can neither be nor be conceived without him, and lastly, that all things have been predetermined by God, not from his free will or absolute pleasure, but from the absolute nature of God, his infinite power. (E1App.)

One can readily see how modern these sorts of conclusions are.[4] There is, first of all, no figurehead God (or gods) looking down upon us and judging what we do, interfering in the world for one purpose or another, or taking offense or pleasure by our actions. There are, in addition, no miracles, no magic, no supernatural events. All that seems in accord with the basic modern scientific spirit of finding causes for each effect, for a universe governed by the laws of nature, and for the idea that all things have, in principle, an explanation.[5] Human beings too would be subject to the "laws of nature" and require that in order for us to understand ourselves, the same scientific approach used to discover anything in nature would be equally applicable to understanding ourselves. Indeed, Spinoza argues that the great mistake has been to "conceive man in Nature as a kingdom within a kingdom" (E3Pref)—that is, seeing ourselves as outside or above the other laws of nature or somehow exempt from them. We are as subject to, and explicable by, the same laws of nature as any object of physics or chemistry and with the same expectation that explanations will be in terms of causes and effects. Appreciating the full implications of this is not so easy as it seems, since our propensity—discussed more below—is to do precisely the opposite.

In fact, for all the talk to this point of Spinoza's humanism, the metaphysics just enumerated seems profoundly *anti*-humanistic. Humanism would suggest the idea of there being something special or unique about human beings that should be explored and celebrated. We should be able to carve out the human realm and see it as somehow distinctive and special, if we are to have a real humanism. To see human beings as simply one object among an infinite number of others, all of which have exactly the same status as being but manifestations of nature in action, seems to accord human beings individually or collectively no more importance to the whole than a gnat or a rock. At least with pre-modern conceptions of humanity we were the highest order of nature, or God's special creation, or the beings with free will or reason that other beings didn't possess, or some such separating set of attributes that distinguished us from other things in nature. In Spinoza's framework the vantage point of the whole seems to imply that we are next to nothing. It would thus seem that the humanistic approach we have taken throughout is not just misleading, but profoundly mistaken. What then is the connection between humanism and insignificance? To that question we now turn.

Insignificance

If our emphasis upon the human in the foregoing chapters is mistaken, we are in good company—namely, Spinoza himself. For immediately after the first book of the *Ethics* (from which most of the preceding was taken), Spinoza moves to his second book "(On the Nature and Origin of the Mind)." Here Spinoza is primarily concerned with the *human* mind just as, when he moves to the third book of the *Ethics* ("On the Origin and Nature of the Emotions") he is primarily talking about the *human* emotions or affects. The fourth and fifth books of the *Ethics* are almost completely focused on the human. At this juncture it is appropriate to remind ourselves of the "worm in the bloodstream" example which serves as the epigraph for this chapter. Here is a fuller selection of that part of the letter from which our opening epigraph was taken.

> Now let us imagine, if you please, a tiny worm living in the blood, capable of distinguishing by sight the particles of blood—lymph, etc.—and of intelligently observing how each particle, on colliding with another, either rebounds or communicates some degree of its motion, and so forth. That worm would be living in the blood as we are living in our part of the universe, and it would regard each individual particle of blood as a whole, not a part, and it could have no idea as to how all the parts are controlled by the overall nature of the blood and compelled to mutual adaptation as the overall nature of the blood requires, so as to agree with one another in a definite way. For if we imagine that there are no causes external to the blood which would communicate new motions to the blood, nor any space external to the blood, nor any other bodies to which the parts of the blood could transfer their motions, it is beyond doubt that the blood would remain indefinitely in its present state and that its particles would undergo no changes ... Thus the blood would always have to be regarded as a whole, not a part. But since there are many other causes which do in a definite way modify the laws of the nature of the blood, it follows that there occur in the blood other motions and other changes, resulting not solely from the reciprocal relation of its particles but from the relation between the motion of the blood on the one hand and external causes on the other. From this perspective the blood is accounted as a part, not as a whole. So much, then, for the question of whole and part.
>
> Now all the bodies in Nature can and should be conceived in the same way as we have here conceived the blood ... Hence it follows that every body, insofar as it exists as modified in a definite way, must be considered as a part of the whole universe, and as agreeing with the whole and cohering with the other parts. Now since the nature of the universe, unlike the nature of the blood, is not limited, but is absolutely infinite, its parts are controlled by the nature of this infinite potency in infinite ways, and are compelled to undergo infinite variations. (Letter 32, to Henry Oldenburg 1665)

Commentators on Spinoza correctly note that this example indicates our very limited perspective on our place within the universe. Not only are we but a small part of the universe, but the vastness of its expanse and its variation of causal forces is actually beyond our comprehension. Our body is, for example, but one of the "particles of blood" flowing through the infinite universe. In addition, the forces acting on that "particle" are themselves infinitely varied and infinitely effective. Thus not only do we have no special place within such a universe, but we seem to be like flotsam on an open sea tossed about by forces to which we can only submit and which we do not comprehend. In addition, it is tempting to read this passage, and others in Spinoza, as suggesting a holism of the sort that swallows up individuality and renders it but a momentary blip in the exertions of one unified expansive substance.[6] Consequently, when we see our place in the bigger scheme of things, our insignificance seems pressing and inescapable.

It is interesting, however, that any problems connected with insignificance are nowhere a part of Spinoza's point in these passages. This absence is not only because his purpose was to explain in general terms the relationship between part and whole, but also because—if the argument of this book has any force—Spinoza does not believe there needs to be a *problem* of insignificance (though he certainly believes in its fact). He does not believe there's a problem because insignificance per se is not something upon which free persons dwell even in the face of a need to recognize it, a point we shall come back to below. Nevertheless, the *matter* or *issue* of insignificance is one we must all face and which suggests two sorts of answers: on the one hand, we can adopt a posture of willful ignorance and a pretense to significance; on the other hand, we can recognize insignificance and seek knowledge. In other words, either one retains some form of the worm's original perspective or one does not. The problem with the former answer is that once the truth about our place has been announced—that is, once the worm knows that the blood is itself only part of a larger whole—it is increasingly impossible to retain the worm's original perspective. Indeed, we thus cannot escape confronting the question of our insignificance even when we choose to deny it!

Correcting the worm's perspective is, of course, what modern science does daily. What was once thought to be the outcome of someone's free will, or an act of God, or thought to be altogether inexplicable is rendered clear in natural causal terms by new discoveries in science, just as Spinoza predicted (E2P49Schol.). Indeed, as soon as we think we have found a safe haven where the worm's original perspective seems to still apply, advances in genetics, neurosurgery, medicine, or some other science immediately calls that haven into question.[7] That we *desire* the haven and, indeed, seek it out, is manifested, for example, in our entertainment. The magical, the superstitious, the inexplicable, the contradictory are all to be found in our films and literature. We are perhaps more drawn to the haven than to our real place in the open sea of our universe. This propensity of ours can turn the recognition of insignificance into the problem of insignificance.

Though commentators are quick to notice the falsity of the worm's perspective on the blood, they seldom mention the worm's natural disposition to view the world around him as he does. Yet it is precisely this disposition that raises the most profound question: is finding out the truth liberating? It is the assumption of every commentator—based on solid evidence from Spinoza's work in everything from his *Treatise on the Emendation of the Intellect* to his *Ethics*—that Spinoza answers this question with a "yes." And while I ultimately agree with that as the correct reading of Spinoza, I also believe that the issue is more complicated than it is assumed to be and that therefore the first response to the question is actually, "no." People tend not to be liberated by the truth, but frightened by it (or at least resistant to it), preferring instead the comforts of the familiar and the "known." The vitriolic reactions to Spinoza's own works are testimony to that truth.

Of course, one is tempted to respond to this last point by suggesting that such people are ignorant and ruled by their passions and imagination and thus not presently capable of appreciating the liberating effects of such knowledge. Those of us who are more educated and learned do, of course, believe ourselves immune from the same sorts of propensities towards the worm's original position. Or are we? Barbarism, superstition, and irrationalism which have been experienced by human kind over the last 100 years (and which still continue) should give pause to anyone that holds to the simple Enlightenment proposition that having the truth about something is in itself liberating. It is even conceivable that the very recognition of the fact of insignificance might alone generate the profound problem of insignificance. Could it be that as our awareness of our true state grows, both the depth of, and propensity for, barbarism grows as well? We intuit this possibility in everything from stories about Frankenstein-type monsters to protests concerning the development of the atomic bomb. We may become complacent about our ability to escape the prejudices of the worm's perspective, because we underestimate the pull upon us of that very perspective. It is a natural one for the worm (and us) because the worm's actual object of intellection is not the universe directly but its own body (E2P13). It is only logical, then, that the perspective would be fundamentally self-centered and local. Consequently, the turning away from truth for the comforts of the worm's original perspective is a possibility for us all, not just those generally moved by their passions and imaginations. Perhaps more accurately, as Spinoza himself tells us (E4P6), we can be overcome by passive emotions however active we are, and we know that activity in one area does not imply it in others. Being "educated" therefore is no guarantee that one escapes the problem of insignificance.

The problem of insignificance is especially exacerbated, but also at least partially explained, by E4P14 where Spinoza says: "no emotion can be checked by the true knowledge of good and evil insofar as it is true, but only insofar as it is considered as an emotion." It would seem, therefore, that simply knowing one's place in the universe is not going to alter one's disposition to seek the haven of the worm's original perspective. And even if we succeed in altering our perspective in one area, our point here has been that we are a "worm" in *every* area of life, not just with respect to cosmology. Hence whether one is involved with rearing children or doing astrophysics, there are infinite modalities with which to contend and thus almost as many ways to take the worm's perspective. The uneducated may not seek the broader view, but the educated tend to believe that their opinions in all areas are equally as enlightened as their opinions in areas of their expertise. This is surely not the case, and Spinoza may have recognized this and addressed himself *particularly* to this educated class of people in his writings, and not to the common sort.[8] Indeed, he reminds us in the very next proposition that, "Desire that arises from the true knowledge of good and evil can be extinguished or checked by many other desires that arise from the emotions by which we are assailed" (E4P15). Spinoza does not qualify this comment by suggesting that some people and not others are exempt from the influence of desires.

As we saw in earlier chapters, ideas carry with them some sort of affective component. That is especially true of true ideas. So why, then, is not truth necessarily liberating? The simple answer is that insofar as we are speaking of the affective side of a true idea, the truth *is* a force for liberation for Spinoza. That is why in E2P14, mentioned above, Spinoza distinguishes the truth from the affective component of an idea. Yet like so many things, that affective component faces numerous contrary affective forces. The idea here is not to reiterate the obvious point that the affective component of a true idea could be overridden, but rather that this is the sort of idea where the overriding is *likely*. Why is this the case? It has to do with the nature of this particular kind of idea. In this case, the idea is that the blood is part of a larger system, as are its parts. Despite appearances to the contrary, this idea about the blood is more on the order of the first level of knowledge than the second or third. If this is so, it would explain why it is so vulnerable to other desires—it really does not carry with it as much power as first appearances might suggest. That an idea *refers* to something big and powerful does not make it a big and powerful idea! One might recall that the first level of knowledge comes from "individual objects" which have come through the senses or "from symbols," such as having "read certain words" (E2P40). These ideas are on the order of opinion. Of course, opinions can be true, but the truth of an opinion does not of itself move it to a higher level of knowledge. For that to occur, the idea must be ordered by reason and integrated with others into a coherent intellectual framework. In that case, the affective component of the idea gains strength from the affective components of the other true ideas with which it is integrated, because there is no conflict between them and each reinforces the others. They form a kind of seamless whole whose collective power may be sufficient to withstand other more passive affections. Integration, however, requires action on our part. To simply hold an idea is, then, largely a passive act.[9]

Thus, to learn that we are but one small part of an infinitely vast and varied universe is to learn a kind of fact. It may be a true fact, but it is not really knowledge and therefore in itself not particularly imbued with the power to liberate. If we are naturally inclined to look at things from our limited perspectives and in ways consistent with what is already comfortable for us, then an idea like this one will have more passive than active properties. Until the idea becomes an integral part of our *activity* as defined in previous chapters, it is subject to being presented in a "fragmentary and confused manner without any intellectual order" (E2P40Schol.2,I). This possibility is so because "whenever the human mind perceives things after the common order of nature, it does not have an adequate knowledge of itself, nor of its body, or of external bodies, but only a confused and fragmentary knowledge" (E2P29Cor.). What does Spinoza mean here by the "common order of nature?" He means what we have just been speaking of. Here are his words:

> I say expressly that the mind does not have an adequate knowledge, but only a confused and fragmentary knowledge, of itself, its own body, and external bodies whenever it perceives things from the common order of nature, that is, whenever it is determined externally—namely, by the fortuitous run of circumstance—to regard this or that, and not when it is determined internally, through its regarding several things at the same time, to understand their agreement, their differences, and their opposition. For whenever it is conditioned internally … then it sees things clearly and distinctly … (E2P29Schol.)

In essence, the new idea the worm has about the blood is simply an isolated fact discovered not by reason and investigation in an integrated way, but rather "fortuitously" through reading, conversation, instruction, or word of mouth. These sorts of ideas—and if we're honest, many or most of our ideas fit this category—are essentially passive in nature. We hold them, but they do no real work for us. Imagine then a world in which we are constantly bombarded by various versions of the worm's revelation about the true nature of the blood. That is our modern world. We cannot escape the question of insignificance. It becomes a problem for us because we hold all these various confirmations of Spinoza's picture of the universe in precisely the passive form in which they were delivered—discrete, unconnected, albeit true facts. In this form, their affective consequence can only frighten and threaten, not liberate, when we merely imagine their meaning. Hence we have the problem of insignificance. It is, as we have suggested, a problem whose cause is also a clue to its solution.

Immanence

We saw above that God was immanent in everything, and since everything comes from God (or substance or nature) it would seem that we have a serious problem of evil, for God seems to be the cause of evil. It turns out that this claim is itself a "worm in the blood" problem. Consider these words by Spinoza:

> If all things have followed from the necessity of God's most perfect nature, why does Nature display so many imperfections, such as rottenness to the point of putridity, nauseating ugliness, confusion, evil, sin, and so on? But, as I have just pointed out, they are easily refuted. For the perfection of things should be measured solely from their own nature and power; nor are things more or less perfect to the extent that they please or offend human senses, serve or oppose human interests. (E1Appendix)[10]

And also:

> ... for Nature's bounds are set not by the laws of human reason whose aim is only man's true interest and preservation, but by infinite other laws which have regard to the eternal order of the whole of Nature, of which man is but a tiny part. It is from the necessity of this order alone that all individual things are determined to exist and to act in a definite way. So if something in Nature appears to us as ridiculous, absurd, or evil, this is due to the fact that our knowledge is only partial, that we are for the most part ignorant of the order and coherence of Nature as a whole, and that we want all things to be directed as our reason prescribes. Yet that which our reason declares to be evil is not evil in respect of the order and laws of universal Nature, but only in respect of our own particular nature. (TP II, 8)

Like the worm who sees everything from its point of view, we do as well. With the worm's perspective, anything it finds offensive, interfering, frustrating, or destructive of its purposes it calls "evil" or "bad." In reality, however, there are only forces of nature leading to various causes and their effects. The more powerful forces are more "perfect;" the less powerful, less perfect. But there is no perspective from which to regard any of them as defective in themselves. There is, therefore, no evil intrinsic to nature (God or substance). Consequently, if we do not like an effect, we have roughly two ways to consider it: one is to keep the myth of the worm's original perspective alive in some way, so that the event has a meaning that is a function of our own purposes in the world. The other option is to embrace one's role in the newly discovered reality.

The idea that the universe contains "evil" and that God is or is not the cause of it is to take the first option. With this option we manage to maintain the illusion that the endeavors of everything are somehow linked to the value we place upon them. The second option gives our purposes no special status vis a vis the endeavorings of anything else in nature. As we saw a moment ago, however, simply recognizing that the worm's perspective is false and the perspective undergirding the second option is true is not thereby to embrace the second option. It is a necessary step, perhaps, but a step that can only be completed if the recognition can be internalized into activity.

So, what exactly does it mean in general terms to keep the worm's original perspective intact? It means continuing to centralize oneself (or one's own) in principle, but to decentralize oneself in practice. The solution Spinoza seeks, by contrast, is to decentralize oneself in principle, but centralize oneself in practice. In the first case, to place oneself at the center *in principle*—whether it be in cosmology or political theory or in life generally—is to place oneself (or one's circle, perspective, group, species, etc.) in such a position that things outside of oneself cannot be understood without at least some reference to oneself or one's own. Hence, "out there" contains, say, "evil" because *we* find a certain event abhorrent, or because *we* believe God told *us* it was, or because *we* have acted in the wrong way and are being punished, or because they are out to get *us*, and so on. *In practice*, however, one does not see oneself (or one's own) as the source of the benefits or evils that befall one, but as simply one actor among many agents. One's actions may or may not effect change, and there is little certainty about what to do to effect positive change. So the tendency is to seek to exclude, control, or manipulate the factors in one's environment, rather than to use them to enhance and advance one's power to endeavor. In short, one reacts. In the case of evil, we might respond by forgiving ourselves for our weaknesses, or by trying to expunge those elements deemed to be evil, or by apologizing for our sins, or by attempting to manipulate elements so that nothing can act in ways other than what has been dictated by us. What we are not doing is transforming the situation from a bad one into a better one.

By contrast, the second option, and the one that exhibits Spinoza's modern alternative, holds that in principle most of what is "out there" can be understood as operating quite independently of us. Not only are we not the cause of most of what surrounds us, but what does happen must be understood *without* reference to ourselves. Of course, since we're the ones doing the understanding, there's a certain sense in which we are inescapably connected to what we consider. But the idea here is that we see what takes place around us as part of a chain of causes and effects that makes no reference to us and moves of its own accord, unless we are somehow one of the causal elements in the chain itself. The illness from which I am currently suffering, for example, is a function of my being infected by a certain sort of germ or virus which creates the symptoms I am experiencing. Untreated the disease will engender certain sorts of effects. I am not sick because God is punishing *me* for some wrong *I* have done. Rather, I got sick because of my presence next to that person who was sneezing. To say, for example, that the illness was God's will, or my will to embrace "evil," is to insert a break into the causal chain, not another link. As such we really explain nothing. By contrast, in adopting the notion that we are amidst forces and agents whose "purposes" have nothing to do with our own, we become radically decentralized—insignificant if you will—in the scheme of things around us. Yet this is the very perspective that provides the step necessary to centralize ourselves in practice.

Centralizing ourselves in practice means understanding enough of the causal factors operating within our environment in order that we might employ their powers in the service of our own endeavors. This centralization process is one of internalizing or immanentizing within ourselves those causal factors which surround us to the end that their powers act at least partially in the service of our own ends, that is to say, we become active. We have outlined in the preceding chapters what it means to be active. Here our point is that the same conception of immanence we use to explain God's relationship to the universe can serve as a kind of model for our relationship to the forces that surround us. We want those forces to exhibit their effects in ways that makes them seem as if they are flowing from us. That requires us to internalize their characteristics by understanding their natures and then turning that knowledge into actions that originate from within ourselves and not as a reaction to something outside. That is, essentially, what it means to be active. Thus, knowing that my illness is the result of causes outside of myself, and knowing the specifics of those causes, I am able to understand what courses of action I can employ to incorporate the various factors of my environment to effect the sort of changes I desire.

Yet because we are limited by nature, what we can come to immanentize well will also be limited. Indeed, this is the reason why it is not enough to simply purge the worm's original perspective and adopt the new one. There must be endeavoring and not merely recognition. We noted in the preceding chapter that the intellectualist reading of Spinoza seems false to the logic of his philosophy. Consequently, understanding is only truly such through action. Yet in order to gain the power to be active, we must work from the base of the powers we already possess in skills, knowledge, and circumstances. While this last point may seem obvious, it suggests that we cannot simply co-opt everything in our environment. Indeed, it is likely that our decentralized status will make successful integration and activity rather limited in scope. In simple terms, the areas in which one will truly be active will tend to be narrow rather than broad, much like saying one cannot be an expert in everything. For to truly command the powers that surround us and make them our own, our understanding—given our limited nature—must be highly localized. There is only so much we can know and thus do well. As a consequence, an active person may be in a significant state of ignorance and limitation with regard to many things in her environment. Provided that she does not close that environment off by thinking her competence in one area applies ipso facto to others, she can continue to advance her activity. This habit of activity will allow her to recognize her limitations and ignorance and seek ways to diminish them. But in all cases, competence will be localized.

Localized competence does not, however, necessarily spell impotence. Quite the contrary, as we have seen elsewhere, we can significantly expand our power by cooperation with others. But what this realization means is that an effective actor will be one among a variety of actors, not the center of activity herself. The paradox is that the more one limits one's competence in conjunction and coordination with the limited competences of others, the wider the effect of one's competence will be. This last point is true because the clearer we are about our own competences, the clearer we will be about how precisely they can be used in conjunction with other competences. This process of connecting with others is itself a form of immanentizing them, for their powers become one's own (and vice versa). It is why it is possible to speak of such combinations, with respect to their particular combined power, as if they were individuals (E2Def.7). A social situation of diversity, pluralism, anonymity, markets, localized knowledge, and the like would thus be very Spinozistic in the sense of actually increasing the power of the members of it compared with a society that is uniform, homogenous, familiar, regulated, and governed by a general conception of a good for all.[11] That is one of the paradoxes of the problem of insignificance, namely that its solution does not lie in gaining its opposite (i. e., significance).

Immanentization is the solution to insignificance because immanence does not depend upon finding a way to overcome insignificance to succeed; indeed, immanentization cannot successfully *proceed* without the recognition of insignificance, and cannot *succeed* without its reality. In this respect, immanentization is the only possible solution, other than passivity and stagnation which are reactions rather than solutions anyway. We must continually recognize our decenteredness in order to effectively employ the powers that surround us. Once we are under an impression of control, we have in effect attempted to close ourselves off to the truth of our decenteredness. The illusion of control is a suggestion that what is out there is somehow now dependent upon us. It may be true that we are affecting what is around us to a much greater degree. Yet to suppose that we now control something (anything) is to suppose that what we control is no longer subject to forces beyond it and that there is no further horizon to our power. Ridding ourselves of the illusion that there is no further horizon of power is the key to making the procedure of immanentization possible. Ridding ourselves of the first illusion that what we command is beyond any forces outside of it is the key to success, because it keeps us ready to immanentize powers not already incorporated into our actions.

The option of significance is the option to keep these illusions alive. Whether the issue is one of trying to enforce or maintain some favored principle as dogma or an effort to enforce and maintain certain patterns of behavior among members of society, all efforts to solve the *problem* of insignificance by significance,[12] will have, to varying degrees, the effect of denying the truth of insignificance and thus incur the consequences of doing so just mentioned. But as we have been arguing, what modernity now faces that was not true before, is the issue of insignificance. Prior to the advent of modern science and many of its discoveries, we may have been able to live within various myths of significance. To deny it now is to be like the child who covers his eyes with his own hands believing he cannot be seen because he cannot see others. It is a plain denial of the truth, and, as a strategy for coping with that truth, it is one of passivity and vulnerability. The limitations recognized by any single contemplation of our insignificance are real. But when we immanentize the powers around us that define those limitations, our next look outward will be of an entirely different set of limitations, thus putting the previous set of limitations behind us.[13] We cannot escape insignificance (E4Axiom). We can, and must, escape a given snapshot of it.

A particular explanation of something can stop thought by presenting itself as a solution. But with Spinoza there really are no "solutions"—there is rather the increased movement forward to the next pattern of thoughts. Because the universe is infinite in infinite ways, there is always more to be open to. There are, then, no forms, structures, patterns, and so on. that can encompass this openness. We cannot, in other words, "get above it" and circumscribe it. Defined social or intellectual structures are all tempting objectives for us but fundamentally false. All such stopping points are rather but way points. We are called to the continual task of endless immanentizing. There may be rest, but no stopping.

Deep within this framework of analysis, however, is a paradox of momentous practical importance. The paradox is a function of the fact that the strongest motivation for relieving the problem of insignificance is the desire for significance itself. In Spinoza's terms, this desire for significance is rooted in the conatus for self-preservation. Other philosophers, especially in the 18th century, notice a similar tendency as well. In Rousseau the motivation might manifest itself as *amor propre* or in Adam Smith as "the desire to better one's own condition." In all such cases, we endeavor to make ourselves the center of our environment and thus to attain what we have been calling significance. The paradox is that the quest for this significance—despite the falsifying character of the notion of significance itself—is the *necessary* spring for motivating us to manage *in*significance. As we saw in an earlier chapter, that initial spring for our endeavoring is pleasure, which moves us to a "higher state of perfection." It is, of course, our own pleasure and thus our own state of perfection of which we speak. Each stage of perfection, when looked at from our point of view, could be described as a push towards significance. It is not the distributed impartial perspective of a God's eye view of things. It is rather a partial and localized view, one that *does* put us at the very center of things. Now to confuse "perspective" with "motivation" is one of the fallacies of rationalism of which Spinoza cannot be accused, despite his rationalist reputation. The desire for significance (motivation) does not in itself require that one be unfaithful to the truth of insignificance (perspective). And as we noted above, the truth of insignificance does not of itself say anything about any motivation one might have to seek significance.

The instrument of the desire for significance is a powerful one which can spur one on to achievement and breadth of insight. But that same tool can lead to problems of narrowness and control. Thus while the pursuit of significance is necessary in a world of insignificance, it needs an antidote to the tendency it has to close off the reality of insignificance. That antidote is philosophy.

Though philosophers, even great ones, can also be motivated by significance,[14] their role among us should be quite different. As modern society becomes ever more complex and diversified, we have seen the classical role of philosophers diminish. This is as it should be in a

Spinozistic world. To give much of a role to those engaged primarily in universals and abstract considerations when we have just been suggesting that specialization and localization of knowledge are the keys to success, would be fundamentally counter-productive. Philosophers may lament the loss of their centrality as advisors to us all, but that was a role suited to a world of significance where the human center sought a single corresponding human wisdom. The decentered world of modernity has no such need. Indeed, to concretize into practice the universal abstractions of philosophers is positively dangerous, because it inevitably ends in forcing a conformity where diversity is warranted. Although universality is applicable to the laws of nature that govern us, it is not particularly valuable when we're giving consideration to human activity, because activity emanates from within the individual actors, not across them.

Nevertheless, philosophy is absolutely critical to the success of the modern enterprise because philosophy alone can counteract the closing effects that often attend the desire and quest for significance. What philosophy does is keep the recognition of insignificance before us. Without it we would see our successes as solutions and be closed to the next perspective on insignificance we must take to move to the next higher level of perfection. I believe this is at least part of the reason why Spinoza was so eager to address himself to philosophers. Their role in the world he saw coming was changing from one of counselor, advisor, and sage to one of explorer, moderator, and visionary. We see this manifested in other philosophers of the period as well—from Leibniz, to Hume, to Adam Smith—who all saw philosophy as a counterbalance to the potential narrowness of the modern world.[15] In Spinoza's case, the emphasis he gives to the freedom to philosophize in the TTP is a recognition that closing off inquiry is to entrench the worm's original perspective. Here, perhaps, we have a new sort of humanism as well; one that facilitates what is needed for human activity rather than one that appeals to our human vanity.

History

Before closing we need to take a brief look at one other popular endeavor to develop a humanistic philosophy in the modern world. This effort begins after Spinoza, perhaps with Rousseau, and may even be something of a reaction to philosophies like Spinoza's. This alternative perspective is a modern attempt to give significance by radically centralizing the human. It holds that the way to humanize the world is to historicize it. The idea here is that contingency and artifice, which are the essence of human activity, are also the basis for saying that human events are unique and context bound. Those events cannot be understood in terms of a framework of analysis or evaluation that comes from outside of the events themselves or which transcends them. Each event must be understood on its own terms and from frameworks of analysis and meanings internal to the event itself. And while any given event might be compared to other events, it can never be understood in terms of other events or principles brought to them both to explain their natures. Any such principles would have to be either rejected or regarded as themselves being internal to some particular event. There are only trans-situational *categories* of analysis (e.g., class), not trans-situational laws or principles. Since human events are radically unique due to contingencies that are special to the events themselves, this approach elevates the human over anything else in nature and thus can be considered a new sort of humanism.

To get clear about that background framework of historicism in relation to Spinoza's philosophy, we need to notice that Spinoza says the following:

> A thing is termed "necessary" either by reason of its essence or by reason of its cause. For a thing's existence necessarily follows either from its essence and definition or from a given efficient cause. Again, it is for these same reasons that a thing is termed "impossible"—that is, either because its essence or definition involves a contradiction or because there is no external cause determined to bring it into existence. But a thing is termed "contingent" for no other reason than the deficiency of our knowledge. (E1P33 Schol.1)

Contingency, then, is a sign of a defect in our knowledge—our recognition of insignificance, if you will. We call things contingent either because we do not understand their nature or do not understand the causes that brought them about. To appeal to contingency as a means for solving any anxieties associated with insignificance is an effort to gain significance.

In other words, trying to separate off the human by making it a kingdom within a kingdom due to some appeal to contingency is to make a mistake for Spinoza. Thus to the degree that any sense of history depends on the contingent, history too would be a philosophical illusion for Spinoza. Philosophy and history are thus opposed if we take them as philosophies. As one commentator has noted, Spinoza was correct to "distinguish the merely relative truths of history from the truth provided by philosophy."[16] Indeed, our passage from Spinoza above suggests that there are no "relative truths" if such truths are relative because they involve contingency. History and philosophy may, however, be reconciled if we take them to be practices; for the historical perspective is the worm's original one, and the philosophical perspective is the perspective of insignificance so necessary for the advancement of one's perfection. Each relies upon the other and so both are a part of Spinoza's *practical* humanism.[17]

For some commentators, the absence of contingency nevertheless allows us to ascribe history to Spinoza. Consider, for example, this remark by Etienne Balibar: "for Spinoza, nature is also history: a history without purpose, indeed, but not without a process, not without a movement of transformation."[18] History as transformation is certainly consistent with Spinoza's notion of nature being active and transforming itself (*natura naturans*). But Spinoza is equally prone to speak of the *results* of an active nature (*natura naturata*), that is, the outcome a given natural activity has produced.[19] In either case there is nothing especially humanistic about these conceptions taken as philosophical propositions. The human has no special or unique status in such a world. As a practice, however, the transformations that characterize events in the human realm might be especially sought out because of our interest in and our involvement with them.

But the question of whether the perspective of history as process can ultimately be philosophically radicalized needs finally to be considered. By radicalized, we mean the condition where history has itself replaced philosophy. Leo Strauss expresses the point as follows:

> Whereas, according to the ancients, philosophizing means to leave the cave, according to our contemporaries all philosophizing essentially belongs to a "historical world," "culture," "civilization," "Weltanschauung," that is, to what Plato had called the cave. We shall call this view "historicism."[20]

In Plato's allegory of the cave, one of the cave dwellers escapes from the cave into the sunlight and realizes that is where truth is to be found. As a metaphor, the story suggests that philosophy can somehow pull us beyond the merely human realm where we normally dwell to the realm of what is eternal, perennial, transcendent, or ultimately real. History, then, in the sense described by Strauss above, is the idea that we cannot escape our own frame of reference, that all philosophizing is bound by our perspective on things. If there are things beyond the human, we can never know what they are or understand them in any way that moves us outside the human framework within which we must think and act. Presumably this radicalized conception of history would apply to Spinoza's philosophy as well, making his pronouncements about God and nature, causation and effects, necessity and impossibility, and the various other aspects of his philosophy nothing more than an expression of some peculiarly human frame of reference.

Yet, this understanding of history does not give us humanism because it gives the human realm a central or significant place; rather it gives the human the *only* place. We cannot, as classical philosophy hoped, gain any perspective outside of the human from which we might understand the human and non-human alike, and thus give some reason for elevating the human. We are completely locked within a human framework where the only dispute remaining is *which* of the frameworks modernity has developed defines our perspective on things: the cultural, the biological, the psychological, the epistemological, the gendered, the class, or whatever. It is not clear, however, that this conception of history is any real advance over the criticism that might be leveled at Spinoza for not giving the human a special place. For to make everything human does nothing in the end to distinguish or elevate what is human.

In any case, it seems equally clear that this radicalized humanism is not a humanism consistent with Spinozism. But in mentioning this issue our discussion has, perhaps, brought to light two possible forms of humanism. In the one case, there is the humanism that seeks to bracket us off somehow from other things in our universe and give us a special status or value. The historicism defined by Strauss would be the outer limit of this approach. The other sort of humanism is one of empowerment where the object is to find ways of making the activities of human beings more successful. It is this latter sort of humanism that characterizes the humanism of Spinoza. Immanentization is the general model for its success, because it is not the separation of human beings from their universe that matters, but their incorporation within it.

Perhaps it is the case that conceiving of ourselves in the way Spinoza suggests inevitably leads to the anxieties of modern life and the problem of insignificance. Yet it may very well be that the complexities and anonymities of modern life are but manifestations of the very tools necessary for human beings to succeed in their environments. If our nature really is as limited as it seems, we must draw from a wide variety of sources to gain the benefits of their powers and to meet the wide variety of powers we must ourselves confront. We would expect, therefore, the network of interactions to become increasingly complex and well beyond what could be grasped by any one mind or set of them. Perhaps the insignificance of which we have spoken and the call to immanence it requires of us still looks like a diminishment of the human. But to Spinoza it is the combination of insignificance and immanence, in a cooperative effort with others so likewise constituted, that brings us to freedom: "anything that signifies weakness in man cannot be referred to his freedom. Therefore a man can certainly not be called free on the grounds that he is able not to exist, or that he is able not to use his reason; he can be called free only insofar as he as the power to exist and to act in accordance with the laws of human nature" (TP II,7).

Conclusion

"Within the world there can be no exile, for nothing within the world is alien to man."

—(*Seneca*, Consolation to Helvia)

In a famous comparison of immanence and transcendence, Simone de Beauvoir rejects immanence in favor of transcendence.[1]

> Every time transcendence falls back into immanence, stagnation, there is a degradation of existence into the *"en soi"*—the brutish life of subjection to given conditions—and of liberty into constraint and contingence.[2]

Here immanence is a form of stagnation and constraint—an arrested development, if not actual regression. One becomes enfolded in oneself and by failing to reach beyond becomes ever more narrow and self-enclosed. The transcendent, by contrast, represents the outside into which one expands and realizes potentialities. Transcendence thus evokes growth and depth. Needless to say, immanence is the condition to avoid for Beauvoir, whereas transcendence, as the very term suggests, engages our aspirations. Given all that we have said previously,

Beauvoir's attack on immanence deserves a moment of our reflection. Does Spinoza's push to act from within oneself culminate in the kind of stagnated constrained immanence that Beauvoir fears?

Before considering that question we should note that Beauvoir's distinction between immanence and transcendence sometimes gets a more neutral rendering:

> There are two interrelated dynamic aspects of life: it can be maintained only through transcending itself, and it can transcend itself only on condition that it is maintained.[3]

Assuming we are allowed to equate "immanence" with "maintenance," this passage suggests that both immanence and transcendence are *equal* components in a "dynamic" life. This way of looking at the matter is no doubt less disparaging of immanence and thus somewhat more in keeping with Spinoza's own doctrine. Yet what in Beauvoir's way of expressing the matter is actually contributing to the dynamism she mentions? Immanence (maintenance) and transcendence in themselves seem to be more states or conditions than processes. Dynamism, however, suggests motion and process more than it does a state or condition. Our rendering of Spinoza's concept of "activity" in the preceding pages is certainly more dynamic in that sense.

The last passage cited from Beauvoir might mean that the dynamism is the result of a dialectic between immanence and transcendence that arises because of the tension created through their interplay. If so, removing transcendence would, of course, cause the tension to disappear, forcing maintenance into stagnation.[4] Yet transcendence evokes separation and distance from something in marked contrast to the inherent unfolding qualities of Spinoza's one substance or the exertions of an active integrated self. For this very reason it is a term rather foreign to Spinoza's outlook. It is thus unlikely that transcendence is the motive force in Spinoza's way of conceiving activity.

We have suggested that the dynamism in Spinoza is a function of effective integration in contrast to a tension of forces. For Spinoza, things (whether material or ideational) carry with them their own powers of exertion, which then become enhanced or diminished as a function of their effective coordination with other powers populating their environment. There may be dialectical elements that contribute to this process, and in the last chapter we saw—analogously to Beauvoir's notions of maintenance and transcendence—the need for human beings to both centralize and broaden. But we have seen throughout our discussion that the tendency or *conatus* of things is *essentially* assertive for Spinoza and that is the basis from which one must work when considering Spinoza's dynamic notion of activity. In the second chapter we referred to the human psychological dimension of this assertiveness as Spinoza's "positive core," but that locution is not a misleading description of the core of Spinoza's philosophy generally.

No doubt being at the origins of the Enlightenment may have allowed Spinoza a certain optimism about what is possible for human beings, if only they could free themselves from some of the main constraints upon their lives and tap into that positive core. We argued in the last chapter, for example, that responding to issues of insignificance by attempting to control and manage an environment, rather than utilize and incorporate it, is a source of many of the impediments to human advancement. Those impediments share the characteristic of defining for other things or people the scope and limits of their powers, instead of seeking to identify and integrate those powers with one's own. In a similar vein Spinoza does not in ethics have a legislative disposition where the first impulse is to find a rule to regulate the case in question. For that reason, Spinoza is more sympathetic to exemplars, because they are models of successful integration without at the same time demanding uniform imitation; and he is sympathetic to voluntary cooperation, because it does not pre-determine anyone's contribution.

Coordination and unity appear to be more closely tied to immanence than transcendence, because they are very agent centered. Yet there is a hidden feature of this positive core directly connected to Beauvoir's worry about stagnation. Because of the inner driven nature of things in Spinoza's philosophy, the natural propensity of anything is towards expansion and openness, not stagnation, narrowness or closure. In the human case, then, passivity goes *against* human nature. It is one reason why, for example, accounting for a phenomenon like suicide is so problematic within a Spinozistic framework (E3P4–6). Immanence is not, therefore, self-envelopment, but rather its opposite. Passivity is pathology, not normality—however widespread it may be. I believe the insight into the positive character of the nature of being, particularly when applied to the human realm, is what Spinoza brings to us as the essence and promise of modernity and the essence and promise of his humanism.

That promise has been borne out in many ways since Spinoza's day. The expansion of human power brought into being by the modern world would have been inconceivable to inhabitants of antiquity. Humanity has at the same time, however, experienced its most horrific episodes in the modern period. Could it be that the effort to remove the shackles that constrain our power might also unleash immense opportunities for inhumanity? Have not such horrific events undermined at least the optimism of early modernity, if not the modern project itself? In light of our experience in the last few centuries, we must ask a thinker like Spinoza whether the endeavor to purge ourselves of passivity necessarily carries with it some significantly adverse consequences.

By Spinoza's own account, passivity is both widespread and pervasive. Would not that fact alone lead us to expect the development of institutions that, while they may reflect that passivity in themselves, serve nevertheless the purpose of constraining the most destructive potentialities of human irrationality? Is it conceivable, in other words, that certain social structures have evolved precisely to protect the "positive core" from excess though those institutions are in themselves "irrational" or more reflective of our passive rather than active selves?

Religion certainly comes to mind as a possible example of an institution both imbued with passivity but nonetheless of possible service in constraint of the more perverse dimensions of human power. The ever-present character of religion in virtually all societies at all times suggests it may offer something in the way of survival value to human beings. And though we have said virtually nothing about religion here,[5] Spinoza has a lot to say about it, particularly in his TTP. There, of course, he notes the connection between religion and passivity, particularly with respect to the sort of passivity that is tied to the imagination. In addition, there is in that work something of a spirit of liberating us from the more burdensome and stultifying aspects of conventional religion. Religion, then, is a good candidate to explore the question of whether institutions might evolve which both exist as a consequence of the pervasiveness of passivity and yet serve a positive regulatory function.

This sort of issue is not, however, one we can address here, and to answer it would require us to work through the problem of the conceptual incompatibility between passivity and power for Spinoza—something that would take us to the depths of Spinoza's metaphysics and back again. It is perhaps the belief in the incompatibility of passivity and power that marks the essence of Spinoza's optimism. The point to be made at this juncture, however, is a different one, namely, that expansion, openness, and development represent the natural propensity of things in a philosophy such as Spinoza's. Yet Spinoza himself admits that passivity is the statistical norm. How, then, is it possible for passivity to be pervasive if openness and development are our central dispositions? Passivity is, after all, something more than simply a description of the boundaries of our power. If nothing else it represents the effect of other things over us and is thus not a mere boundary condition, but a force in its own right to be confronted. I would like to conclude by suggesting that the raising of such questions about passivity is not in itself a sign of any weakness in Spinoza's philosophy, or of any naïve optimism, provided we regard Spinoza as a philosopher and not merely as an intellectual.

The distinction between philosopher and intellectual can be especially important in the modern era because one of the tendencies of modernity has been to diminish or obliterate any separation between them. To separate them seems to entail driving a wedge between ideas and practice, and modernity has continually struggled to frustrate any efforts to establish such a wedge. Instead, modernity has touted the notion that ideas have consequences, and that truth must be revealed at all costs. As a consequence, falsehood is to be regarded as a direct impediment to our advancement and thus is intolerable, even unjust. These characteristics of modernity indicate a strong reluctance to allow any gap in principle between theory and practice.

Spinoza would seem to be an early advocate of such views. As mentioned a moment ago, Spinoza's apparent quest to purge us of superstition and to advance the freedom to philosophize seems to be one of the main messages of the TTP. Moreover, some of our remarks in earlier chapters of our discussion here could be read as calls to reform on Spinoza's part in areas such as politics, psychology, and ethics. Most importantly, though, would be the doctrine that because ideas have their own inherent power for action, Spinoza's philosophy could be seen—and indeed has been seen—as implying that there actually can be no separation between ideas and practice. But if there can be no separation between ideas and practice, the prevalence of passivity would seem to tell against the notion of there being a "positive core" where our disposition is towards activity.

If one approaches the problem as an intellectual, then, it is difficult to distance Spinoza from the charge of naïveté, optimism and possibly contradiction, given all that has taken place in modernity since Spinoza's time. Intellectuals, however, formulate ideas with information, trends, and practices that are present and visible. They articulate what everyone sees but are unable to articulate for themselves. The tension between the inherent openness and hence the power of ideas on the one hand, and pervasive passivity and irrationality on the other, appears to make it impossible to ever claim that openness, growth, and activity are in fact the central propensities of our nature. There is simply too much evidence to the contrary.

But if we approach our question from the standpoint of a philosopher, there need be no inherent conflict. Philosophies seek underlying causes and propensities. They articulate not what people are already disposed to believe or do, but precisely what is not so visible to even careful observers of current beliefs and practices. That there is no separation between ideas and practice is itself a philosophical claim. That claim, however, in no way implies that there is therefore no separation between the *doing of philosophy* and practice. Indeed, if philosophy really does probe underlying causes and propensities, we should be suspicious of a philosophy that is readily accepted, or which simply captures the ideas of its age, or which provides the steps needed for practical reform. We expect philosophies to be in some deep and important way ageless. They lead us to insights no matter what era calls upon them for reflection. The cost of achieving such insights may be effective practicality.

One of Spinoza's ageless insights, then, and one of his main gifts to the nature of modernity, is that despite the evident limitations upon our mental and physical powers, there is immense human potential. That insight is a philosophical one and thus remains true whether most people are passive or not. It will remain true even if we retreat into barbarism. Indeed, it is a kind of paradox that beings so obviously limited and subject to forces of passivity can nevertheless accomplish so much. It is because beneath the surface of all the pain, suffering, setbacks, limitations, irrationalities, and the like, there is indeed a propensity towards activity and therefore tremendous possibility for growth and advancement. It is, as we have claimed, in the very nature of us.

Once the insight was known and appreciated, modern intellectuals turned it into a doctrine of progress. But Spinoza's philosophy is not a program for reform where we can identify the steps to advancement, or even a philosophy of progress that projects necessary forward development. Spinoza gives no hint that paths of regression can be permanently closed. Furthermore, when he does explicitly put a program of reform together, such as in the TIE, it tends to be procedural and to emphasize the importance of philosophy. Keeping open the avenues to the central insights are what philosophy and the philosopher can do. But philosophy does not thereby confuse the inseparable link between ideas and practice with a necessary link between the philosopher and practice. The latter can lead to the destructive ideologies of which the modern world has been so full. The former leads to understanding.

If we are prone to openness, growth, and advancement, then the person able to give expression to those dispositions will achieve the sort of transcendence Beauvoir recommends. Our ability to look outside of ourselves and our circumstances and to link ourselves up with others doing likewise is the central component to our success. We have argued that the ability to do just that depends upon a form of immanence, an inner active integrity that is possible for us all. Spinoza's humanism consequently looks out from what is human to the world; not from the world to what is distinctively human as other humanisms do. But immanence does not only describe the source of this modern activity, but its terminus as well. The modern person will not find satisfaction in the collectivities, institutions, practices, social patterns, or cooperative ventures in which transcendence demands she participate. That satisfaction will come through the very immanence that makes looking beyond oneself possible. Being part of another is not a substitute for being whole with oneself. The modern world offers an infinite variety of things of which one can be a part, and the need to reach beyond ourselves means they can all call to us. The return to one's own immanence, therefore, is the most difficult lesson of modern life. Perhaps that is why it is so rare.

Notes

Introduction

1. Jonathan I. Israel, *Radical Enlightenment: Philosophy and the Making of Modernity 1650–1750* (Oxford: Oxford University Press, 2001), p. vi.
2. Ibid. pp. 11–12.
3. Of course, he may have done so because he felt it was the realm ultimately most knowable for us. Aaron Garrett notes something along these lines in Aaron V. Garrett, *Meaning in Spinoza's Method* (Cambridge: Cambridge University Press, 2003), p. 218.
4. Paul Kashap, "Some Recent Works on Spinoza's Thought," *Journal of the History of Ideas*, Vol. 38, No. 3, (July–Sept. 1977), p. 545.

Chapter 1

1. Oakeshott cites Hobbes's own introduction to the Latin edition of *Leviathan*: "This great Leviathan, which is called the State, is a work of art; it is an artificial man made for the protection and salvation of the natural man, to whom it is superior in grandeur and power." Michael Oakeshott, *Hobbes on Civil Association* (Indianapolis: Liberty Fund, Inc., 1975) (HCA) p. 77.

2. Michael Oakeshott, "The Activity of Governing," in *Morality and Politics in Modern Europe*, Shirley Robin Letwin (ed.) (New Haven: Yale University Press, 1993), p. 22.
3. Oakeshott, HCA, p. 84. Spinoza says that nature as a whole "is nothing other than the power of all individuals taken together" *Tractatus Theologico-Politicus* (TTP) Ch. XVI. See also Lee C. Rice, "Spinoza on Individuation," *The Monist*, Vol. LV, No. 4 (October 1971).
4. Oakeshott, HCA, p. 82.
5. Ibid., pp. 20–21.
6. Steven B. Smith, *Spinoza, Liberalism, and the Question of Jewish Identity*, op. cit., p. 122.
7. Ibid., p. 144.
8. Using the word "encouraged" rather than "protected" makes the proposition false in my view, which would be consistent with my point. Consequently, "protected" begs fewer questions about what I am saying.
9. I use these passages to similar effect in "Liberalism and Virtue," in *Public Morality, Civic Virtue, and the Problem of Modern Liberalism*, T. William Boxx and Gary M. Quinlivan, eds. (Grand Rapids, Michigan: William B. Eerdmans Publishing Co., 2000), pp. 58–60.
10. In the preceding paragraph of the TP Spinoza uses "civitas" rather than "imperium," which may indicate this distinction. I am not convinced, however, that the case can rest on this alone, because I am not confident the terms have such consistent usage.
11. Den Uyl, Douglas J., *Power, State and Freedom: An Interpretation of Spinoza's Political Thought*, Van Gorcum 1983, Ch. 5.
12. Lee C. Rice points out to me that terms do not always have consistent meanings in the *Ethics* either. Some of the remarks I make about the passages in the *Ethics* on issues related to politics should bear this out. Rice also cautions that one should not read this statement as meaning that one can avoid reading the *Ethica* and still get Spinoza's views on politics. I would endorse this caution and do not mean this point to imply that one could read one without the other.
13. Michael A. Rosenthal, "Tolerance as a Virtue in Spinoza's *Ethics*," *Journal of the History of Philosophy* Vol. 39, No. 4 (October 2001) p. 549.
14. Such texts are often "contradicted" by others, which refer to the same subjects. One might, for example, take the passage about the arts and sciences to mean government promotion in that area. That's refuted directly by TP VIII 49.
15. Spinoza follows these words by linking equality to freedom, suggesting that Spinoza in a significant way did not abandon the democratic ideal in this later work and also suggesting that the non-democratic regimes he discusses work to the extent that they retain some significant element of democracy.
16. He is like Machiavelli, however, in distinguishing the public from the private and thus having two tiers in that sense.
17. There may appear to be an ambiguity in Spinoza that may lead one to conclude that Spinoza actually does the reverse of what I have suggested above, namely that he

ends up virtually equating morality and politics. We are told, for example, that "sin is inconceivable except in a state" (TP II, 19) and that the sovereign power of the commonwealth is to decide what is "fair or unfair, moral or immoral" (TP III, 5). Such views are not found only in the TP, but also in the TTP as well, for example, Chapter XVI. In this connection we can keep in mind our distinction between ethics and morality. It should also be noted, I believe, that Spinoza in these contexts is establishing the practical basis for the functioning of morality, namely the relevant base of power. For a discussion of power in Spinoza, see Steven Barbone, "Power in the *Tractatus Theologico-politicus*" in Bagley, *op. cit.* pp. 91–109.

18. The first one to make this point is H. F. Hallet, *Creation, Emanation, and Salvation*, (The Hague, Martinus Nijhoff, 1962), esp. Chapter 10.
19. Rosenthal, *op. cit.*, p. 549.
20. *Power, State and Freedom*, *op. cit.*, Ch. 5.
21. I believe this is also an adequate response to those who might argue that the "effect" of Spinoza's politics is the same as the "effect" of a politics intentionally sought by the same means. The latter would call for additional measures should the end sought fail to be achieved. The former would not.
22. Rosenthal, for example, succumbs to it when he equates the state to an individual: p. 554, note 29.
23. The most important scholarly statement to this effect is found in Alexandre Matheron's, *Individu et communaute chez Spinoza* (Paris: Les Editions de Minuit, 1969). Matheron also makes the point as a subject of controversy in interpreting Spinoza's political theory in a book review: *Studia Spinozana* (Walther & Walther Verlag) Vol. 1, 1985, p. 425.
24. *Ibid.*, p. 8.
25. "Perfectionist ethics and non perfectionist politics" is a phrase later used by my co-author Douglas Rasmussen and me as the subtitle of our book, *Norms of Liberty* (Pennsylvania University Press, 2005).

Chapter 2

1. This chapter in large measure utilizes a paper I gave at a conference on the "Philosophical History of Strengths and Virtues" at the University of Pennsylvania in September. 2004. Besides *Character Strengths and Virtues: A Handbook and Classification*, Christopher Peterson and Martin E. P. Seligman, eds. (Oxford: Oxford University Press, 2004) henceforth CSV, the works with which I am most familiar are *Authentic Happiness*, by Martin E. P. Seligman (Free Press, 2002) and *Learned Optimism*, also by Martin E. P. Seligman (Free Press, 1990).
2. This is not to suggest that there are not divergent paradigms of physical health. Statistical normalcy is one way of determining what is "normal" and "healthy," but not the only way. It seems to be, unfortunately from my perspective, the way

used in CSV to determine the central virtues. But this is not the place to take on that model.
3. *Authentic Happiness,* op. cit., p. 249.
4. Seligman (*Learned Optimism,* p. 14) notes that "the conventional view [of health] omits a major determinant of health—our own cognitions. Our physical health is something over which we have far greater personal control than we probably suspect. For example:

- The way we think, especially about health, changes our health.
- Optimists catch fewer infectious diseases than pessimists do.
- Optimists have better health habits than pessimists do.
- Our immune system may work better when we are optimistic.
- Evidence suggests that optimists live longer than pessimists".

5. *Authentic Happiness,* op. cit., p. 102.
6. Ibid., p. 104.
7. Ibid., p. 107.
8. Ibid., p. 112. As Descartes once suggested, "emotion" is an ambiguous concept when considering its role in relation to mind and body, since it is seemingly neither or both. As discussed in note 15 below, emotion is probably not a good term of translation in Spinoza. We need a term that straddles the mental and physical because it is a term that is referring in many ways to the relationship of them both. What is usually translated as "emotion" does function that way in Spinoza. And while Seligman and positive psychology may wish to relegate the term exclusively to the realm of pleasure, I believe they too need a term that straddles both dimensions. This is why I'm particularly drawn to Spinoza's use of "passive" and "active" emotions or affects and why I believe positive psychology makes a similar conceptual turn.
9. Given the Spinozistic orientation of this book, I find the term "gratification" somewhat wanting as a term for what positive psychology wishes to include under this conception. The reason Seligman gives for making the distinction (ibid., p. 111)—namely that English does not discriminate between pleasure and gratification—is precisely the reason for abandoning its use. Gratification is much too passive and "after the fact" for it to function as a term describing the enactment of personal strengths and virtues. Yet actually coming up with a good alternative is not so easy. English does not easily handle a eudaimonistic conception of happiness and thus has no real concept of what we are later (following Spinoza) going to call active emotions. It seems to me that following the usual translation of *eudaimonia* as "flourishing" and then referring to positive psychology's "gratifications" as "flourishings" would be a better way to proceed. However, because "gratification" is already in use, I shall not attempt to reform that usage here.
10. Ibid., p. 119.

11. A wonderful and interesting discussion of this full range is given by Antonio Damasio in *Looking for Spinoza: Joy, Sorrow, and the Feeling Brain* (Orlando: Harcourt Books, 2003). Damasio is especially interested in the biological and organismic role of feelings, desire, and emotions. Our analysis here is certainly influenced by Damasio's discussions.
12. Ibid., p. 30. Actually he prefers to think in terms of homeodynamics because of the more active and adjustment oriented nature of the process rather than the static.
13. There are, in fact, many terminological disputes surrounding all these terms. The term "emotion" is a translation for *affectus*, which many would argue is somewhat misleading. It is likely that the best consensus on a translation would be simply "affects" rather than emotion. We have remained with the historically more common "emotion" here because it fits better with the language of positive psychology.
14. Damasio, op. cit., pp. 12–13. The last sentence of the paragraph cited notes that these endeavors are engaged unconsciously. This, of course, does not preclude the conscious—indeed it can function through it—and that, as stated, is our focus here.
15. As Spinoza notes, this is not in terms of persistence through time but persistence through endeavoring. See the last paragraph to the preface to E4.
16. Seligman, *Authentic Happiness*, Ch. 3.
17. Ibid., p. 224.
18. Ibid., p. 116. I would have said "self-consciousness" rather than simply "consciousness," which is what I take the meaning to be here.
19. We learn earlier that "nothing can happen in the body without its being perceived by the mind." (E2P12) and moreover that "the object of the idea constituting the human mind is the body" (E2P13).
20. "The conatus with which each thing endeavors to persist in its own being is nothing but the actual essence of the thing itself." (E3P7).
21. Incidentally, this is a reason why not everything one discusses in Spinoza has to be discussed *sub specie aeternitatis* all the time. Spinoza is perfectly willing to discuss human freedom even though, even by his standards, there is no possibility of complete freedom.
22. There are a number of good general introductions to Spinoza that discuss these themes. For example, Henry Allison, *Benedict de Spinoza: An Introduction* (New haven: Yale University Press, 1987); Stuart Hampshire, *Spinoza* (Penguin Classics, 1993); Genevieve Lloyd, *Spinoza and the* Ethics (London: Routledge, 1996). For a more detailed analysis, consider Jonathan Bennett, *A Study of Spinoza's Ethics* (Cambridge: Cambridge University Press, 1984), Ch. 11. Especially influential on my own perspective is Lee C. Rice, "Emotion, Appetition, and *Conatus* in Spinoza," *Revue Internationale de Philosophie,* Vol. 31 (1977) pp. 101–116.
23. Not exclusively or even most importantly, however. There is the "third kind of knowledge" which is the highest and deepest for Spinoza and is not the usual sort of discursive reasoning (E5P25).

24. I would endorse the following statement from Yirmiyahu Yovel: "Spinoza claims in the *Treatise on the Emendation of the Intellect* that once the rational process has been launched, it becomes self-enhancing and even, in a sense, self-engendering, because its exercise amplifies and further accelerates the power of reason. At this stage, so Spinoza seems to hold, the external causes which had triggered the rise of rationality are internalized and transformed into reason's own self-causality operating within the individual and *as* the individual. In other words, reason as a self-engendering, self-enhancing natural power gradually takes over from the external inducements which have initially provoked it to arise in the individuals." Yirmiyahu Yovel, "Incomplete Rationality in Spinoza's Ethics," in *Spinoza on Reason and the "Free Man,"* Yirmiyahu Yovel and Gideon Segal, eds. (New York: Little Room Press, 2004), p. 16.

Chapter 3

1. Don Garrett, "Spinoza's Ethical Theory," in *The Cambridge Companion to Spinoza*, Don Garrett, ed. (Cambridge, 1996), p. 297. Garret notes later (p. 313, note 35) that Spinoza bears little resemblance to deontology by his lack of use of terms like "duty" and "obligation" and, I might add, "autonomy." Still, Garrett notes that Spinoza links ethics to "reason" in a way not totally unlike Kant, and of course, other similarities that may exist are being explored here.
2. Rice and I together make the same point. See Douglas Den Uyl and Lee C. Rice, "Spinoza and Hume on Individuals," *Reason Papers*, No. 15 (Summer 1990), p. 102ff.
3. Lee C. Rice, "Spinoza's Notion of 'Tenere' in His Moral and Political Thought," in *Ethik, Recht un Politik bei Spinoza*, Vortrage gehalten anlasslich des 6. Internationalen Kongresses der Spinoza-Gesellschaft vom 5. bis. 7. Oktober 2000 an der Universitat Zurick, p. 150.
4. "Good" and "evil" are terms related to our limitedness, partiality, and inadequacy. I cannot avoid using them entirely, but this caveat about their use should be noted.
5. Willi Goetschel, *Spinoza's Modernity, op. cit.*, p. 51.
6. Lee C. Rice, Spinoza's Notion of 'Tenere' in "His Moral and Political Thought," *op.cit.*, p. 150. For further elaboration, see also his "Spinoza's Ethical Project" in *Agora Papeles de filosofía*, Vol. 21, N° 1, 2002, pags. 77–92.
7. I am not completely satisfied with the locution of "ethics" versus "morality" though it does capture something of what I'm saying here and no better distinction comes to mind.
8. Spinoza tells us exactly this when he says, "if it *were* equally in our power to live at reason's behest as to be led by blind desire, all *would* be led by reason, and *would* order their lives wisely" (TP II, 6).
9. Another reason the exemplar works well for Spinoza has to do with the third level of the good and the third level of knowledge discussed below.

10. "Spinoza and Hume on Individuals," *op. cit.* A number of aspects of this chapter are elaborations of themes suggested in that one.
11. The *Tractatus Theologico-Politicus* was the first and major political work available in Spinoza's lifetime. The *Tractatus Politicus* was written towards the end of his life and was never finished or available during his lifetime.
12. In *TTP* XVII we are told that that "he who reigns in the subjects' minds holds the most powerful dominion" and that "nothing can so captivate the mind as joy springing from devotion."
13. One might wish to consult, *Piety, Peace, and the Freedom to Philosophize*, Paul J. Bagley, ed. (London: Klewer, 1999) for essays on this topic including one of my own.
14. CSV, pp. 29–30.
15. Ibid., pp. 51–52.
16. In discussing the "problem" with virtue ethics (Ibid., p. 88), positive psychology notes that virtue ethics may fail because it does not tell us exactly what to do and because it cannot resolve conflicts among virtues. It might thus need to be combined with another theory of moral conduct to solve these problems, but this is not the concern of positive psychology because its concern is simply the role of the virtues in a healthy psychological life. In this positive psychology seems to want to separate the healthy psychological life from the moral life or morality, and I have noticed this distinction in a number of places. It is, in my view, a rather un-Spinozistic distinction. Successful living *is* moral living for Spinoza. There are no other realms to appeal to or which capture the "moral" beyond that. That is Kantianism. Saying this neither implies that there may not be issues to consider with such a view. There are. Nor does it imply that principles and duties are thereby absent. All that has to be examined. But it cannot be the case, as it is so often, that the Kantian starting point of the moral order being distinct and separate from successful practice is simply assumed at the outset.
17. Damasio notes (*op. cit.*, p. 281) that William James resisted Spinoza's sunny view of life and his "healthy-mindedness" because such cheerfulness ignored too much the tragedy of death. See below.
18. Also E4P35Cor.1.
19. It is interesting that Spinoza responds to the negative with the positive: "he who strives to overcome hatred with love is surely fighting a happy and carefree battle" (E4P46Schol. and see E5P10Schol.).
20. Though this is not completely accurate, it is not too misleading to say that the active person of E3 becomes the virtuous person in E4 where ethics is more explicitly addressed.
21. Positive psychology has seemed to ally itself fairly clearly with Aristotle on this issue. While wisdom is one of the possible signature strengths, there is little mention of reason or knowledge when it comes to discussing authentic happiness. Indeed, there is a kind of Aristotelian turn in positive psychology which begins to emphasize strength of character and paths to wisdom rather than knowledge itself.

Neither "reason" nor "knowledge" has a separate index entry in either *Authentic Happiness* or *Learned Optimism*, for example. We may, therefore, have a definite departure of the ways between Spinoza and positive psychology.

22. By the same token, in positive psychology there seems to be little interest in reason, knowledge, or truth. Provided we have habituated certain dispositions, it matters not what they are about or with what they may be connected. It may be that "character strength" alone is sufficient for positive psychology to function, at least in a therapeutic way.
23. One of the central differences between the two thinkers perhaps centers on teleology, which Aristotle has plenty of, and Spinoza little, if any. The teleological element would give a boundary to meaningful activity and thus give more of a place to character traits. Without teleology, power or activity is perhaps unlimited in itself. Humans seek to expand their power without limit, even though as finite beings unlimited power is not possible. Still, the boundaries of that power are unknown and thus there are no limits to the legitimacy of that power in Spinoza as there may be in Aristotle.
24. See, for example *Politics* Book 2, Ch. 2.
25. The propositions (35–40) which are literally central to Part IV of the *Ethics*, and which I am claiming are transition propositions from knowledge and good at level two to level three, are essentially about internalizing the powers of others with oneself for effective flourishing for all. It is here that one might seek to develop a perfectionistic political interpretation of Spinoza, an interpretation I believe to be mistaken but not implausible, as we noted in chapter 1. For my part, when Spinoza does talk about politics in these propositions, he drops away from reason and back to affection (e.g., E4P37Schol.2), so I believe, as we saw, that the case cannot be made from these passages that Spinoza has a perfectionist politics.
26. This is no doubt at least partially because we do in fact live in social situations and are subject to rules, customs, and practices that we have no part in making.

Chapter 4

1. Ursula Goldenbaum, "The Affects as a Condition of Human Freedom in Spinoza's *Ethics*," in *Spinoza on Reason and the "Free Man," op. cit.*, p. 149.
2. It is useful in this context to look again at E3P9&Schol.
3. Hobbes states that "by liberty, is understood ... the absence of external Impediments" (*Leviathan*, Ch. XIV). Of course, we could solve this issue semantically and say that "liberty" for Hobbes was unimpeded motion, and "freedom" could be something else. However, in Hobbes there is still less of an interest in a distinction between active and passive actions than there is in Spinoza.
4. For example, see Jonathan Bennett, *A Study of Spinoza's Ethics* (Indianapolis, IN: Hackett, 1984), pp. 364–369.

5. Margaret D. Wilson, "Spinoza's Theory of Knowledge," in *The Cambridge Companion to Spinoza, op. cit.*, p. 132.
6. Steven B. Smith interprets it exactly this way in *Spinoza, Liberalism, and the Question of Jewish Identity* (New Haven: Yale University Press, 1997), p. 138, and then gives this centrality in Spinoza's political philosophy, contra our own position as discussed in chapter 1.
7. In this connection, for example, see Moira Gatens and Genevieve Lloyd, *Collective Imaginings: Spinoza, Past and Present* (London: Routledge, 1999), Ch. 3.
8. Nevertheless, we believe that Spinoza is wrestling with a real problem of modernity, later considered again by Hume and most forcefully by Adam Smith. That is the problem of the role of philosophy in a world moved primarily by sentiment and practical action. How successful Part V seems to be in this regard is an important question. We believe that the general framework for a successful answer is better laid out here than in, say, Smith. On the other hand, we also believe that Spinoza is less successful than Smith in understanding the nature of the problem and the sorts of concerns it contains. We shall look at some of these issues a bit more in the next chapter. For Smith on this issue see Charles Griswold, *Adam Smith and the Virtues of Enlightenment* (Cambridge: Cambridge University Press, 1999), esp. chapter 2; and my review of Griswold's book in *The Journal of the History of the Classical Tradition* Winter 2001.
9. But even in Spinoza's early life he was a man of practical affairs in his father's business.
10. Rebecca Goldstein, *Betraying Spinoza* (New York: Schocken Books, 2006), p. 162.
11. Ibid., p. 186.
12. We might recall from an earlier chapter that positive psychology saw a meaningful life as "using your signature strengths in the service of something larger than you are."
13. Seligman, *Authentic Happiness, op. cit.*, p. 260.
14. Ibid., p. 268.
15. *Op. cit.*, p. 274.
16. The third kind of knowledge is essentially the integration of universal and particular. Spinoza defines it thusly in E2P40Schol.2: "this kind of knowledge proceeds from an adequate idea of the formal essence of certain attributes of God to an adequate knowledge of the essence of things." See in this connection E5P24.
17. Damasio, *op. cit.*, p. 283.
18. An excellent example of this perspective done well can be found in Moira Gatens and Genevieve Lloyd, *Collective Imaginings: Spinoza, Past and Present* (London: Routledge, 1999), p. 80ff.
19. Spinoza seems fairly clear that we understand best at the level of particulars however much we may need to also construct the general. Referring to his rather abstract proof in *Ethics*, that everything is a function of God, Spinoza says: "that proof, although legitimate and exempt from any shadow of doubt, does not so

strike the mind as when it is inferred from the essence of each particular thing which we assert to be dependent on God" (E5P36Schol.).
20. Spinoza's famous "worm in the bloodstream" example is discussed extensively in the next chapter.

Chapter 5

1. Gilles Deleuze also uses this term in much the way I do in the abstract, though our uses and conclusions in many cases would be opposed. See *Spinoza: Practical Philosophy* (San Francisco: City Lights Books, 1988) translated by Robert Huxley, for example, Ch. 6.
2. We know, of course, of ancient theories that took exception to this view, such as the Pythagorean.
3. Willi Goetschel notes, "That Substance as a whole, however, appearing as it does under the aspect of body and mind, remains beyond any totalizable discursive grasp. As understanding garners knowledge through the aspect in which a particular object manifests itself, it can also grasp things in their dual aspect: as individual entities on the one hand and as partial manifestations of the interconnected yet unfathomable ground of being on the other. In this way, the relationship between particular and the universal is expressed ontologically as both difference and identity" (*op.cit*, p. 27).
4. It should be noted that I am not really allowing for the concept of "postmodern" to factor into our picture here. I do not mean by modern what is sometimes limited to the sensibilities of the 17th and 18th centuries, nor to what was true for much of the 20th century but is being altered by new perspectives. This is because what Spinoza is saying is equally relevant today. The postmodern emphasis on power is to be found, for example, in Spinoza (as we have seen) and has been emphasized by such "postmodern" writers as Delueze and Negri. Especially with respect to the two main categories of this chapter, there is no datedness to Spinoza or reason to relegate him to a period of history now surpassed.
5. There are, these days, challenges to some of the picture being painted here—namely in quantum physics and chaos theory. The somewhat Newtonian picture being drawn is certainly subject to these sorts of exceptions. The interesting question from a Spinozistic perspective is whether these apparent anomalies to orderliness are bits of counter-evidence to the theory or whether we are simply seeing something of the nature of the other attributes and their modes in Spinoza's infinite system.
6. We have chosen not to read Spinoza in this way throughout, but the metaphysical issue of individuality is too involved for a treatment here. Suffice it to say that although individuality is a relational concept for Spinoza, as per Lemmas 4–7 of E2, relationalism does necessarily diminish the separate individuality of the relata.

7. The great effort, of course, to find a permanent place for that haven is Kant's division of the universe into the noumenal and the phenomenal realms where the latter realm is the empirical world we experience and subject to the laws of science, whereas the former is a realm outside the bounds of science.
8. In the Preface to the TTP, for example, he addresses himself to the philosophic reader: "Such, learned reader, are the topics which I here submit for your consideration. ... To others I seek not to commend this treatise, for I have no reason to expect them to approve it in any way." Of course, this section of the Preface is optimistic that the learned can move outside of the worm's perspective. My point is not that the likelihood is not greater with that class of people, but rather that it is still quite possible that they may remain like the worm in so many areas.
9. The second level of knowledge, while active, is not necessarily *open* to immanence even though it has captured some. It captures only the universal side of immanence but not the particular side and the connection between them. This is why theorists often lack practical wisdom. The intellectual is thus prone to a kind of hubris of supposing his model is the real world and holding it up as a way of encompassing it all. There is an increasing degree of immodesty. This contrasts with Spinoza's *Ethics,* which has the sensibility of increasing modesty as one moves through it. The third level is not a program of modeling the universe but one of moving within it. The universal is immanentized in the particular in such a way that neither is understood in itself but in terms of the paths of activity one may now follow. There is no sense of trying to grasp the whole; only one of moving with it.
10. This is the concluding part of the appendix. There is a great deal more that precedes it which makes the same point.
11. In this respect the market order of specialized cooperators is the social/political expression of these insights. Spinoza's social project is very Hayekian in this sense. Many commentators today (e.g., Negri, Deleuze, possibly Martinez and Goetschel), however, endeavor to pull Spinoza in the other direction—towards some kind of collectivism or socialism. Needless to say, the argument here is against that reading. We would hold that communitarianism and socialism are the political expressions of refusing to face insignificance. Nonetheless, these authors are among the best in appreciating Spinoza's sense of power and the importance of immanentization.
12. Keep in mind here our earlier distinction between the issue of insignificance and the problem of insignificance.
13. In philosophical terms, modernity might also be thought of as the continual effort to overcome dualisms inherited from the past. These include subject/object, mind/body, self/others, community/individual, master/slave, and the like. Each side of the dualism represents an ontological separation or a kind of limitation upon the other side. In a world of significance, such as one might find in antiquity, the dualisms are managed either by subordination of one to the other, or by equilibrating the tension that exists between the two sides. In particular cases, for example,

classical realist epistemology, there is a movement toward undermining the dualism between knower and known.
14. See, for example, Matthew Stewart, *The Courtier and the Heretic: Leibniz, Spinoza, and the Fate of God in the Modern World*—a wonderful account of a philosopher moved by the desire for significance (Leibniz) and one who was not (Spinoza).
15. In each case, there was fear in the narrowing effects of the modern world. Among Scottish Enlightenment thinkers it was a concern about the problems of "faction." In addition, Adam Smith in his educational philosophy sought to counteract the effects of narrowness brought on by modern conditions of specialization (See, WN Bk. V). Leibniz, for his part, wanted special science fairs to produce the same broadening effects upon the people.
16. Steven B. Smith, *Spinoza, Liberalism, and the Question of Jewish Identity* (New Haven: Yale University Press, 1997), p. 62.
17. Smith also notes that for Spinoza, "history is intended to fulfill an emancipatory function." Ibid., p. 63.
18. Etienne Balibar, *Spinoza and Politics*, translated by Peter Snowdon (New York: Verso 1998), p. 122. Change for Balibar is dialectical and here that conception is applied to nature as a whole. Just prior to the statement cited here Balibar also gives support to our point in footnote #10.
19. This is a standard reading, but it is not clear that the text of the *Ethics* always supports it. See E1P29Schol.
20. Leo Strauss, *Natural Right and History* (Chicago: University of Chicago Press, 1965), p. 12.

Conclusion

1. Simon de Beauvoir, *The Second Sex* (New York: Vintage Books, 1989), H. M. Parshley translator and editor. The distinction is used in various places throughout the work. The distinction has to do with gender relationships, specifically the subjugation of women by men and the specific forms of life each has traditionally adopted. Here I have abstracted the distinction out of its original context to make the point about Spinoza I want to make. I do not imply, of course, that I am in any way representing Beauvoir's position in the use I make of her distinction.
2. Ibid., p. xxxv.
3. Ibid., p. 13.
4. That is essentially her point about what men have historically done to women.
5. Some of my own views relevant to this question can be found in "Power, Politics and Religion in Spinoza's Political Thought," in *Piety, Peace, and the Freedom to Philosophize, op. cit.*, pp. 133–158. The works of all the authors in this volume are worth consulting, and there is additionally a large literature on Spinoza on religion.

Bibliography

Allison, Henry. *Benedict de Spinoza: An Introduction*. New Haven: Yale University Press, 1987.
Balibar, Etienne. *Spinoza and Politics*, Peter Snowdon, translator, New York: Verso, 1998.
Barbone, Steven. "Power in the *Tractatus Theologico-politicus*" in *Piety, Peace, and the Freedom to Philosophize*, Paul J. Bagley, editor. Dordrecht, Netherlands: Kluwer, 1999.
Beauvoir, Simone de. *The Second Sex*, H. M. Parshley, editor and translator. New York: Vintage, 1989.
Bennett, Jonathan. *A Study of Spinoza's Ethics*. Cambridge: Cambridge University Press, 1984.
Curley, Edwin. *The Collected Works of Spinoza*. Princeton, NJ: Princeton University Press, 1986.
Damasio, Antonio. *Looking for Spinoza: Joy, Sorrow, and the Feeling Brain*. Orlando: Harcourt, 2003.
DeBrabander, Firmin. *Spinoza and the Stoics*. London: Continuum, 2007.
Deleuze, Gilles, *Spinoza: Practical Philosophy*, Robert Huxley, translator. San Francisco: City Lights, 1988.
Den Uyl, Douglas J. *Power, State and Freedom: An Interpretation of Spinoza's Political Thought*. Assen, Netherlands: Van Gorcum, 1983.

Den Uyl, Douglas J. "Power, Politics and Religion in Spinoza's Political Thought" in *Piety, Peace, and the Freedom to Philosophize*, Paul J. Bagley, editor. Dordrecht: Kluwer, 1999.

———."Liberalism and Virtue" in *Public Morality, Civic Virtue, and the Problem of Modern Liberalism*, T. William Boxx and Gary M. Quinlivan, editors. Grand Rapids, MI: Eerdmans, 2000.

———. "Autonomous Autonomy: Spinoza on Autonomy, Perfectionism, and Politics," *Social Philosophy and Policy*, Vol. 20, No. 2, Summer 2003.

———. "Spinoza and Oakeshott" in *The Intellectual Legacy of Michael Oakeshott*, Corey Abel and Timothy Fuller, editors. Charlottesville, VA: Imprint Academic, 2005.

Garrett, Aaron V. *Meaning in Spinoza's Method*. Cambridge: Cambridge University Press, 2003.

Garrett, Donald. "Spinoza's Ethical Theory" in *The Cambridge Companion to Spinoza*, Don Garrett, editor. Cambridge: Cambridge University Press, 1996.

Gatens, Moira, and Genevieve Lloyd. *Collective Imaginings: Spinoza, Past and Present*, London: Routledge, 1999.

Goetschel, Willi. *Spinoza's Modernity: Mendelssohn, Lessing, and Heine*. Madison, WI: University of Wisconsin Press, 2004.

Goldenbaum, Ursula. "The Affects as a Condition of Human Freedom in Spinoza's Ethics" in *Spinoza on Reason and the "Free Man,"* Yirmiyahu Yovel and Gideon Segal, editors. New York: Little Room, 2004.

Goldstein, Rebecca. *Betraying Spinoza*. New York: Schocken, 2006.

Griswold, Charles. *Adam Smith and the Virtues of Enlightenment*. Cambridge: Cambridge University Press, 1999.

Hallet, H. F. *Creation, Emanation, and Salvation*. The Hague: Martinus Nijhoff, 1962.

Hampshire, Stuart. *Spinoza*. New York: Penguin, 1993.

Israel, Jonathan I. *Radical Enlightenment: Philosophy and the Making of Modernity 1650–1750*. Oxford: Oxford University Press, 2001.

Kashap, Paul. "Some Recent Works on Spinoza's Thought," *Journal of the History of Ideas*, Vol. 38, No. 3, July–Sept. 1977.

Lloyd, Genevieve. *Spinoza and the Ethics*. London: Routledge, 1996.

Martínez, Francisco José. *Autoconstitución y libertad: Ontologia y politica en Espinosa*. Barcelona: Anthropos Editorial, Rubí, 2007.

Matheron, Alexandre. *Individu et communaute chez Spinoza*. Paris: Minuit, 1969.

Negri, Antonio. *The Savage Anomaly*, Michael Hardt, translator. Minneapolis: University of Minnesota Press, 1991.

Oakeshott, Michael. *Hobbes on Civil Association*. Indianapolis: Liberty Fund, 1975.

———. "The Activity of Governing" in *Morality and Politics in Modern Europe*, Shirley Robin Letwin, editor. New Haven: Yale University Press, 1993.

Peterson, Christopher, and Martin E. P. Seligman, editors, *Character Strengths and Virtues: A Handbook and Classification*. Oxford: Oxford University Press, 2004.

Rice, Lee C. "Spinoza on Individuation," *The Monist*, Vol. LV, No. 4, October 1971.

———. "Emotion, Appetition, (??) and Conatus in Spinoza," *Revue Internationale de Philosophie*,Vol. 31, 1977.

———. "Spinoza's Notion of 'Tenere' in His Moral and Political Thought" in *Ethik, Recht un Politik bei Spinoza*, Vortrage gehalten anlasslich des 6. Internationalen Kongresses der Spinoza-Gesellschaft vom 5. bis. 7. Oktober 2000 an der Universitat Zurich.

———, and Douglas Den Uyl. "Spinoza and Hume on Individuals," *Reason Papers*, No. 15, Summer 1990.

Rosenthal, Michael A. "Tolerance as a Virtue in Spinoza's Ethics," *Journal of the History of Philosophy*, Vol. 39, No. 4, October 2001.

Seligman, Martin E. P. *Learned Optimism*. New York: Free Press, 1990.

———. *Authentic Happiness*. New York: Free Press, 2002.

Shirley, Samuel. *Spinoza: Complete Works*. Indianapolis: Hackett, 2002.

Smith, Steven B. *Spinoza, Liberalism, and the Question of Jewish Identity*. New Haven: Yale University Press, 1997.

———. *Spinoza, Liberalism, and the Question of Jewish Identity*. New Haven: Yale University Press, 1997.

Stewart, Mathew. *The Courtier and the Heretic: Leibniz, Spinoza, and the Fate of God in the Modern World*. New York: Norton, 2007.

Strauss, Leo, *Natural Right and History*. Chicago: University of Chicago Press, 1965.

Wilson, Margaret D. "Spinoza's Theory of Knowledge" in *The Cambridge Companion to Spinoza*, Don Garrett, editor. Cambridge: Cambridge University Press, 1996.

Yovel, Yirmiyahu, editor. *Desire and Affect: Spinoza as Psychologist*. New York: Little Room, 1999.

———. "Incomplete Rationality in Spinoza's Ethics" in *Spinoza on Reason and the "Free Man,"* Yirmiyahu Yovel and Gideon Segal, editors. New York: Little Room, 2004.

Masterworks in the Western Tradition

Nicholas Capaldi, *General Editor*
Stuart D. Warner, *Associate Editor*

This series is intended to exhibit for the intelligent reader why certain authors, texts, and ideas are the key to understanding ourselves and our relation to the world as well as each other. The series answers the question: What is the core of western civilization? Each volume (approximately 100–150 pages) will be written about one author and will explain the background to the author's work, the major philosophical ideas—especially their moral and political implications, the influence of the author on subsequent thought, the major issues identified and left unresolved, and the on-going importance of the author's ideas. Approximately one third of each volume will focus on a major work of that author. Each volume will have a bibliographic essay. While there are many series on major thinkers, no such series is designed to respond to this theme of the core of Western Civilization and to do so in a uniform format with some consideration of how individual authors relate to other authors.

For additional information about this series or for the submission of manuscripts, please contact:

> Acquisitions Department
> Peter Lang Publishing
> 275 Seventh Avenue, 28th floor
> New York, New York 10001

To order other books in this series, please contact our Customer Service Department:

> (800) 770-LANG (within the U.S.)
> (212) 647-7706 (outside the U.S.)
> (212) 647-7707 FAX

Or browse online by series:

> www.peterlang.com